SONG OF THE PHOENIX

THE HIDDEN REWARDS OF FAILURE

"There is a certain bird which is called a Phoenix. This is the only one of its kind and lives five hundred years. And when the time of its dissolution draws near that it must die, it builds itself a nest of frankincense and myrrh and other spices into which, when the time is fulfilled, it enters and dies."

Clement I
A.D. 90

In Clement's description, after the phoenix expires in flames, another phoenix arises from the ashes and flies to Egypt, where it places the remains of the old phoenix on the altar of the sun. In the mythologies of Turkey, Persia, China, and the Christian world, the phoenix represents regeneration, transformation from death to life.

Just before the phoenix dies, it begins to sing — the only time in its lifespan of five hundred years that its voice is heard. The song of the phoenix is so beautiful that all creation stops to listen. Then, still singing, the phoenix is burnt to ashes.

The crisis of the phoenix is its burning, and out of the ashes comes the rebirth. Crisis can be seen, therefore, as a positive aspect of change.

SONG OF THE PHOENIX

THE HIDDEN REWARDS OF FAILURE

JOHN LORD with JEFFREY WOLD, M.D.
INTERVIEWS BY JENNIFER WALKER LORD

BERKSHIRE HOUSE, Publishers
STOCKBRIDGE, MASSACHUSETTS

We gratefully acknowledge permission from the following publishers and individuals to use excerpts from the following authors: *The Fellowship of the Ring*, J. R. R. Tolkien, 1988, Houghton Mifflin; *Habits of the Heart*, Robert N. Bellah, 1985, Univ. of California Press; *Selected Poems and Two Plays*, William Butler Yeats, 1962, Collier-Macmillan; *These Branching Moments, Odes by Rumi*, transla. John Moyne and Coleman Barks, 1988, Copper Beech Press; excerpt from *Collected Poems, 1909-1962* by T. S. Eliot, copyright 1936 by Harcourt Brace Jovanovich, Inc. and copyright © 1964, 1963 by T. S. Eliot; Interview with Buckminster Fuller, New Dimensions Radio; *When Grapes Turn to Wine, Versions of Rumi by Robert Bly*, 1983, Robert Bly.

Quotes from the following authors were derived from *Life 101* by John-Roger and Peter McWilliams, © 1990 by Prelude Press: Ralph Waldo Emerson, Rainer Maria Rilke, Henry Miller, Don Marquis, Thomas A. Edison, Mary Pickford, William James, David Augsburger, Woody Allen, Isaac Bashevis Singer, Joan Baez, Thomas Merton, Theodore Roosevelt, C. G. Jung, Henry A. Kissinger, Fred Astaire, William Butler Yeats, T. S. Eliot.

Designed and edited by David Emblidge and Virginia Rowe.
Cover design: Catharyn Tivy
Typesetting: Eileen M. Clawson, Custom Typography
Printing: Baker Johnson, Book Printing & Binding

Library of Congress Cataloging-in-Publication Data
Lord, John, 1954-
Song of the phoenix: the hidden rewards of failure / John Lord with Jeffrey Wold; interviews by Jennifer Walker Lord.
p. cm.
Includes bibliographical references.
ISBN 0-936399-15-5 : $16.95
1. Failure (Psychology) I. Wold, Jeffrey, 1947- . II. Lord, Jennifer Walker. III. Title.
BF575.F14L67   1992
155.2'5—dc20   90-84843
                                                        CIP

ISBN 0-936399-15-5

First Printing
Printed in the United States of America

To our parents

Herbert and Martha Lord
Mickey and Lillie Walker
Roger and Rhoda Wold

CONTENTS

FOREWORD

WHO HAS NEVER FAILED at a job, in a relationship, on some project, or in the basic process of trying to make a life? Failure is an unavoidable piece of life, and yet when it happens we tend to see it as an aberration and a surprise. We may have fantasies of never failing again, even though we know, especially as we grow older, that perfect success in anything is an illusion. It seems a simple thing, then, to take a more sympathetic look at failure, inquire into its mystery, and even consider how it might make a contribution to life and to personality.

But it's not so simple. It's even revolutionary to give failure an open hearing, perhaps because our culture is so thoroughly youthful in its spirit, so given to idealism, ambition, and success. Most self-help books and inspirational guides tell you how to succeed, not how to benefit from failure. In fact, our insistence on success is so strong as to be anxious and exaggerated — signs of a feeling that has little depth and shadow. Failure, of course, is the shadow of success — indeed, the deep shadow made by lofty ambitions. Such shadow experiences often contain the emotions and thoughts needed to give substance and soulfulness to our anxious and obsessive intentions.

John Lord has done us the great service of telling his personal story of failure, as well as gathering the stories of others who are sensitive to failure in their lives. I urge the reader not to move too quickly from story to interpretation. It is extremely useful to contemplate these stories, find ourselves in them, and wonder at the mystery these concrete, graphic instances of failure bring to our very notion of what human life is about.

The moral or interpretation given by the authors of these stories, including John Lord's tale of disasters, I take to be part of the stories, as much the individual's myth as the narrative he or she relates. It's too easy to hear a story about failure and take a quick lesson from it so we can be spared our own future failures. It's more instructive to learn how to hold the emotions and fantasies in failure, to allow them to work on our hearts, transforming us with saving us; giving us depth, a less innocent point of view, a wounded intelligence, and an awareness that human intention and ambition are incomplete without the incursion of failure from below.

C. G. Jung once noted in passing that the psyche moves most in those places where it is weakest. Along the same lines, John Lord makes the interesting observation that etymologically failure is a deception. I would imagine that it is our ambitions and expectations that are deceived — fortunately, I would say, just as the medieval theologians describe the failure or fall of Adam and Eve as a "fortunate mistake." For, failure contains the mystery of our lives that is locked and bound by our wishes for success. When we fail, we discover certain truths about ourselves and about life that otherwise would remain hidden and out of reach.

Success, taken as an absolute, is a Promethean attempt to steal the fires of spirit from the gods. Failure restores piety towards fate and destiny, allowing some influence in life beyond our own egotistic intentions. It isn't so much that we learn from our failures, as that we reorient ourselves by means of the very emptiness and threat that failure admits into the heart. Our far-reaching spirit, whether it is naturally ambitious or is a reaction to experiences of suppression, is tempered by failure, and ripened. True success in life can only be achieved when the soul has been seasoned and is ready for the complexity of human experience. Success and failure play equal roles in this preparation.

It may be tempting to reduce the stories of failure you read here to easy explanations and simple lessons. But failure is always complicated, and the stories of these lives could offer a wide variety of interpretation. What is behind the many fantasies of achievement and success in the first place? Is a particular failure the end result of some obsessive longing, the acting-out of a need of the soul that has gone unheeded? The stories invite us to explore many dimensions of the myth of failure. Therefore, I recommend that this book be read with reflection and contemplation, rather than with the wish for an answer to a common problem. This is the book's pleasure and its gift: the opportunity to contemplate our own foolishness, which many religious traditions teach as the way toward the deepest kind of self-discovery.

THOMAS MOORE
Author and Psychotherapist

ACKNOWLEDGMENTS

IN THIS BOOK we use the metaphor of a journey. The writing of the book was also a journey — undertaken first by one person, and joined along the way by others. When it became clear that I needed to examine not only my experience, but the experiences and wisdom of others, and I realized that other people's stories would be a vital part of this book, Jennifer Walker Lord, my wife and partner in our vocational counseling and workshop practice (which we call The Life Project), stepped in. She took responsibility for gathering and writing the stories and exercises that you find throughout this book, and her help has been invaluable. All along we have had an important dialogue partner in Dr. Jeffrey Wold, a psychiatrist for twelve years at the Austen Riggs Center in Stockbridge, Massachusetts, and now in private practice. As the book progressed we depended heavily on Jeff for his contribution and guidance.

Many others joined us on the journey. Some were authors from whom we've drawn liberally both in spirit and in word. Men and women from all over the United States and Canada, having experienced failure, were moved to share their stories with us so that others might benefit from them. This journey, started by one, became a parade before we were done.

Many people made the writing of this book not only possible, but rewarding and enjoyable, offering inspiration, advice, support, resources, and, at times, casseroles and childcare.

First and foremost, we are especially grateful to those who contributed their stories, some of which are included in the text. All have helped to shape and refine our reflections on the failure experience. In every case, we were enormously enriched by getting to know these individuals, and we value greatly the spirit in which they shared their experiences and wisdom.

Our gratitude goes also to both Kim Garlinghouse, who cheerfully donated her computer for months on end so that we could pull the final manuscript together — and to Lewis Randa and the Peace Abbey for the use of equipment and space, which helped to make a big project manageable.

Many others were very generous with their ideas, critical advice, love and encouragement, among them Mary Wold, Peter Lund, Stephen Marini, Dan Brewer, Katherine Kallis, Bobbi Miner, Joanna Ross, and the members of our spiritual support group at Newton Highlands Congregational Church. We have also been inspired by the example set for us by David Gershon and Gail Straub in their work on personal empowerment.

We thank our friend and publisher/editor David Emblidge, who encouraged the writing of this book. And, finally, we want to express our appreciation for the interest, good humor and patience our children Ben and Katie Lord who, without complaint, made room in their lives for "the book."

Creating this book has ultimately been a collaborative effort. Without assistance from those we have mentioned here, the book could not have been written, or if it had, it would never have been read.

"But everything seems so neat and orderly we'd never guess that your lives are falling apart."

Drawing by Ziegler; (c) 1991
The New Yorker Magazine, Inc.

INTRODUCTION

Do not be too timid and squeamish about your actions. All life is an experiment. The more experiments you make, the better. What if they are a little coarse, and you may get your coat soiled or torn? What if you do fail, and get fairly rolled in the dirt once or twice? Up again; you shall never be so afraid of a tumble.

RALPH WALDO EMERSON

The purpose of life is to be defeated by greater and greater things.

RAINER MARIA RILKE

When you fail, you learn things. Have you put that in the book . . . in grown-up words?

ADVICE TO THE AUTHOR FROM
HIS EIGHT-YEAR-OLD SON

The road goes ever on and on
Down from the door where it began.
Now far ahead the road has gone
And I must follow if I can
Pursuing it with eager feet
Until it joins some larger way
Where many paths and errands meet.
And whither then?
I cannot say.

BILBO BAGGINS
[from *The Fellowship of the Ring*
by J. R. R. Tolkien]

A CHALLENGE TO THE READER

YOU ARE READING a book on *failure*. We have written one. We have something in common. Not having all the answers to what failure is or why it happens binds us together. The spirit of discovery drives us onwards.

Exploration is difficult. It involves leaving familiar surroundings and traveling to places that may seem strange or even hostile. The accustomed ways of doing things — or of thinking about things — don't apply with quite the same reliability. You may feel thrown back on your own resources perhaps against your will. It can be frightening. André Gide said that "one doesn't discover new lands without consenting to lose sight of the shore for a very long time."

But a journey — even one that you didn't want to make and would have avoided if you could — doesn't have to be entirely bad. We have all had experiences of finding to our surprise that there are times when unexpected help arrives at just the right moment. Strangers whom you meet along the way turn out to be friends and helpers in disguise. And one of the advantages of being thrown back on your own resources is discovering that you *have* resources.

You have a wealth of talents, interests and abilities that have long remained hidden beneath a cleverly conceived but not entirely authentic persona. Nevertheless, in a moment when failure stops you dead in your tracks, you may feel that a journey is the last thing you want. You may feel like putting your foot down and saying along with Bilbo Baggins in J. R. R. Tolkien's *The Hobbit*, "No more adventures!"

For many, however, the important explorations in life are inevitable; there comes a time when staying home becomes more troublesome, more anxious and more frustrating than setting out, regardless of what may lie ahead. The journey through failure is one of that sort: staying home with failure, digging in and refusing to see where it might lead you, wears a little thin after a while.

When the feeling of failure becomes overwhelming, the sense of collapse (for failure is essentially the collapse of *something*) is a signal that you have arrived at a crisis. Crisis is limiting: it directs attention to itself and fixes it there. The bone breaks, it hurts so much that you can't think of anything else. Crisis is monotonous: it makes us believe that the crisis itself is all there is: no variation, no let up. Crisis is enervating: it forces the senses into a steady state of dull alarm. Yet, for most of us, crisis cannot last. It is unstable. There is a line in the Tao Te Ching which states: "He who is sick of being sick is not sick." Eventually, most of us get sick to death of crisis, and we begin to feel the stirring of an impetus within that calls us away from such limiting circumstances. The longer crisis persists (and for some people, a failure experience may stretch out over several years), the more insistent this impetus becomes, until, finally, screwing up whatever courage we may have left, we turn our faces to the road ahead and begin our journey.

So what sort of exploration are we speaking of when we say that failure, if given its due, may take us somewhere new? First of all, it is a journey through changes.

Have you ever lost a job, gone through a divorce or some other painful separation? Or a business failure or bankruptcy? Almost everyone gets a turn. All these are changes which can be devastating. If you are right now going through a crisis such as these, it may be comforting to read in these pages the stories of others who have been in similar straits and have come through, not only as good as before, but different than before and better. Along this journey there are stages, stations of the cross, if you will, that are common to the experience of many others. You will find in these accounts, trials — and victories — that may closely mirror your own. At the same time, a mirror can only show a reflection, not the thing itself. Your life as you live it is your own. The poem at the end of this chapter, by the 13th-century Persian poet Rumi, speaks of learning from the myths but urges us "not to be satisfied" just with the stories of others: we must go further until we discover the stories each of us owns. It is by comparing and *contrasting* your story with those included here that you may find a spur that jabs you awake or a pearl of wisdom meant only for you.

Finally, this business of digging down into the dark, subterranean territory that is failure's home ground is a journey of transformation. The stories of people we interviewed showed us over and over that those who could open themselves to the reality of their experience made an invaluable discovery. If they allowed themselves to be transformed — shaped, molded, renewed — by the things that had happened to them previously, in failure, they gained a power and ability to work a similar transformation in their new experiences — their attitudes, their relationships, their economic circumstances and, ultimately, even the course of events. Does this sound grandiose, as though it's the stuff of melodrama with heroes and villains? The journey through and out of failure corresponds in many ways to the great quests of mythology which Joseph

Campbell, in his *Hero With A Thousand Faces*, describes as follows:

> *"The standard path of mythological adventure of the hero is the magnification of the formula represented in the rites of passage: separation-initiation-return. A hero ventures forth from the world of common day into a region of supernatural wonder: fabulous forces are there encountered and a decisive victory is won: the hero comes back from this mysterious adventure with the power to bestow boons on his fellow man."*[1]

You needn't think that our book expects you to become a hero, literally, in the classical sense. We use the word "hero" in the way that Campbell did: "We are each of us heroes in our own story." Each of us plays the leading role, for better or for worse. As we prepared this book, as we looked into our own lives and compared notes with others, we began to see that there were common patterns and features in our stories that confirmed the appropriateness of our mythological metaphors of heroes and epic adventure. There were shadow experiences, and many spoke of challenges and perils. But there were also, in many of these stories, accounts of sudden and unexpected discovery. A gift may indeed have been won: either in the recognition of specific individual "giftedness" or talent or, more generally, the gift of greater self-awareness and circumspection that is the reward of all travelers who explore uncharted waters over the horizon. Having gone out there — or, in failure, more likely *down* there — you may see things the others you left behind haven't even dreamed of as yet. And, once back, many of our interviewees felt a call to share their newly recognized gifts with others, responding enthusiastically to our queries, eagerly seeking to pass along what they learned to any who might benefit from their experience.

This book is an attempt to help our storytellers fulfill that charge and to help you formulate the story of your own failure, to make it resonate with insight and usefulness.

But let's keep our perspective and humility even as we celebrate the courage of our storytellers whose lives *did* change. This book offers no panacea to help you build up within yourself a guaranteed way to avoid failure, to achieve or sustain success. This book is not a set program that, if followed religiously, promises a specific outcome. In fact we do not even wish for you that failure will never again come your way. General Douglas MacArthur, a man who knew extraordinary triumphs and defeats, on and off the battlefield, said, "There is no security on this earth, there is only opportunity." And indeed this book does not promise anyone that life can be lived in a rose garden, immune from failure. We believe, and our interviewees told us repeatedly, that failure has its own proper, legitimate, healthy place in the course of everyone's life: failure has that paradoxical quality of never being placed on the guest list but always adding something positive when it crashes the party.

ABOUT THE STORIES

The interviews included in this book were all given to us by people who were eager to recount their stories, especially if their stories could help others. Although many of the people who shared their lives with us were comfortable having their identities revealed, several felt the need for anonymity for professional reasons. To simplify matters, we changed the names and identifying details of everyone's story (unless otherwise indicated) so that all may remain anonymous.

In the course of our research, we sent a questionnaire out to a long list of friends, associates and acquaintances, and were amazed at how many took the time to fill them out thoughtfully and send them back. Later, several "authors' queries" were published in newspapers, and this was our major source of interviewees. For weeks after the notices appeared, we would continue to receive calls and letters. Some people — total strangers — poured out their life stories on paper. Often we would find messages on the answering machine, such as the one left by an older gentleman: "Hello, I am calling in response to your request for information for your book on failure. I have had many failures in my life, accelerating in seriousness, and all in all I am very satisfied with my life. I would be happy to be interviewed."

One fellow called several weeks after a notice appeared in his local paper. He said, "I have to confess. When I saw the notice in the book review section I was really interested but decided not to respond and I threw the paper away. Then I reconsidered and went to retrieve the paper and tore your notice out. I've been carrying this thing around in my wallet for over two weeks. Finally today I got up the nerve to call."

People seemed drawn to this subject — and whether they simply filled out a questionnaire or eventually sat down with us for an interview, we frequently heard how helpful it had been to look consciously at these experiences of failure. Our files are bulging with stories of failed marriages, jobs, careers, health, relationships, and of broken self-images. They are also filled with stories of hope, determination, understanding, compassion, and faith. More often than not, several of these themes appear together within single stories.

There was nothing especially scientific about our research. We proceeded impressionistically — seeking to discern and then to recreate the realities of our respondents' stories. In meeting these people, we have been immensely enriched. We feel great respect for their life journeys and have been inspired by their stories. We hope we have captured something of their essence on these pages.

A ROAD MAP TO THE BOOK

It has been our plan from the beginning that there should be two benefits at least that all our readers will gain from reading this book: one, comfort and encouragement, and two, practical advice.

We have included as many different perspectives on the problem of failure as possible without sacrificing clarity. Most respondents and interviewees focused their stories of failure on work, career, jobs, and finances — perhaps typical in a culture where success and failure and many other values are so often defined by their superficial or external manifestations. Inevitably, however, one part of life affects other parts, and so, throughout these stories, which often begin as tales from the business world, you will find extensive and revealing comments about failed family and romantic relationships as well as failed health and the like. Our inclusive ambition is that any individual will feel that he or she is part of a wider phenomenon, a universal experience, which if not talked about openly, is nevertheless deeply felt by people of all ages in all places at all times. No one needs to compound the misery of failure with the loneliness of feeling that "this has never happened to anyone but me."

Once finished, the book should provide fresh insights and an expanded view of life in which to consider any failure experience. In order to accomplish this, we have organized the book in such a way that it may be used as a personal workshop for exploring the different dimensions of failure.

How does one become **an** authority on *failure*? We have enjoyed a good many laughs about this question while writing this book. On the one hand, one of us (Dr. Jeffrey Wold), a psychiatrist, can claim the authority that comes from day in and day out experience with his patients and clients, who bring to him their personal problems, many of which are colored by the theme of failure. But what of this book's primary author, John Lord? ... From where does John's authority on failure derive? From his own experience of several failures in business, the arts, and in relationships related to these events; from an extensive study of relevant literature ranging from the technical to the poetic; from listening carefully to the stories about failure this book's interviewees were eager to tell; and finally from having carried through the difficult exercise — which we recommend to you — of writing down as honestly and thoroughly as possible the story of his own experience with failure and where it came from in his life. That story is in the Appendix of this book. We hope you will read it.

Chapter One, *The Problem and Promise*, offers an overview of the issues involved, positive and negative, the trials and the rewards. Additionally, you will find here certain key concepts that should be helpful for transforming failure into meaningful success. We should add that these concepts were not our own invention, but arose out of the common experience of those we interviewed. Some you will find helpful, some you may not. Feel free to pick and choose.

Chapter Two, *Failure and Society: Values, Causes, Meanings* is an attempt — from a lay observer of the state of things in the world — to place failure in the context of bigger changes going on around us: social breakdown, political confusion, economic disintegration, and the like. Such an overview may be a bit ambitious for a little book. However, it is precisely these great social changes that are redefining everything we must consider in coming to an understanding of what success and failure mean today to the interior lives of individuals.

In Chapter Three, *Failure and the Individual: The Stages of Failure*, we look more closely at the elements and some of the stages of failure as they were related to us by our respondents. This includes a look at the precipitating event, and the way we react to the onset of failure: physically, psychologically and spiritually. The chapter ends with a reflection on themes of death and rebirth.

Failure, when it occurs, affects many different aspects of life: some more than others, perhaps, but all to some extent. Chapter Four, *Three Common Areas for Failure*, looks at school, work and relationships.

Chapter Five, *Failure as Threefold Process: Crisis, Stuckness, Breaking Free*, stresses the dynamics and the evolution of failure beginning with an *initial crisis* where one may feel that "the ground is opening beneath me," to an *in-between state* (called "stuckness"). Here the individual lives in a habitual adaptation to crisis. The *third stage* ("crisis-in-crisis") is when crisis itself changes and begins to come to its natural end.

The final chapter, Six, *Failure as Resource: Transformation and Empowerment*, presents important aspects in the transformation of failure into insight and meaning, with all the opportunities for a rich, new life and liveliness to which that change gives birth. Here, the hidden reward of failure is discovered not as something outside of ourselves which we must struggle to acquire, but rather as a powerful force within which it is our task — and our privilege — to reveal, to tame, to use.

The Appendix begins with John Lord's story. This is offered to give you a more extended example of how, in one case, that of the book's primary author, the failure experience evolved and how one person made sense of it. The particulars here are not the real issue, rather it is the themes, the common feelings about failure that begin to emerge: this is meant as grist for the mill of your imagination as you review the earlier chapters that analyze the phenomenon of failure in a broad sense.

Several chapters conclude with Exercises. We hope you will try them out, not only because the exercises are stimulating, but also because doing them greatly facilitates progress toward discovering in concrete and personal ways what failure's hidden rewards can be.

A WORD ABOUT "VOICE" IN THIS BOOK

You are holding a multi-author book that in one sense speaks in a chorus of voices (the interviewees, the writers we quote . . .); and in another sense is a book written by one fellow — John Lord — with help from two teammates, Dr. Jeffrey Wold, as consultant-author, and from Jennifer Walker Lord, as chief interviewer-author. Here, in the Introduction, the team speaks collectively to you about the making of this book. From Chapter One onwards, the voice (the "I") in the text is that of John Lord, except, of course, in the interviews themselves.

HOW TO GET THE MOST OUT OF THIS BOOK

There are two important things to remember if you want to get your money's worth from this book: One, make the material your own and two, do those exercises.

As you read through the chapters, take the time to consider which ideas have a particular relevance to you in your situation. Watch for those that strike a sympathetic chord, or cause a twinge or a grimace. Whenever this occurs look out for special significance. It may take some reflection. The exploration of failure involves the consideration of certain concepts — the nature of experience, for instance — that are so basic that we usually take them for granted. Since many of us are not in the habit of thinking about ideas so fundamental, we may need to invest a little extra energy in getting a clear understanding of what is being discussed. In any case, in every case, use your own experience as the backdrop for the material. Allow our ideas to be projected against your own and watch for whatever meaning emerges. In the final analysis, it will be your own life experience that will be your primary resource in making use of what we have to offer.

As for the exercises, we recommend that you set aside a certain time each day and try to protect that time as your opportunity to read and reflect and complete the assignments. As you go along, also take the opportunity to look back on the work you have done to date. Are the answers you gave a while ago the ones you would give today? If you were to answer differently, what would you say now? Are there similarities or patterns beginning to emerge? What significance do these patterns have for you? Are they a sign of a developing direction to your life that you had overlooked? Or perhaps they indicate a type of behavior you would like to change.

You might wish to set up a journal to keep track of insights about failure as they appear; or, try drawing, or scribbling, playing with crayons or paints. One never knows what will come of such exercises. Expect nothing but stay open. Some time ago, when we were attending a workshop on self-empowerment, we were asked to "meditate on paper" using colored markers. One of us came home with four different drawings, each meaningful in itself, but when we placed one on top of the other and held them up to the light, a pattern emerged that was more telling than any of the individual drawings had been alone. So we recommend — especially to those left-brainers who "never do this sort of thing" — that you give it a try: you just might end up watching your own transformation unfold before you on paper!

HOPEFUL ANTICIPATION

Most of all, expect a change. As we will discuss in detail later on, failure and failing are not static. If there is failure in your life, it is a sign that something is changing. The more deeply felt the experience of failure, the more profound the change. As new information presents itself, your mind will continue to work on it — waking and sleeping —

until the information has been synthesized with all that went before. When it is ready, but not before, this new synthesis will appear to you. Watch for it. Anticipate this moment. You may be sure that it will occur. You may be just as sure that when it does, it will be full, pregnant, rich with new and exciting possibilities. Carl Jung, a pillar of modern psychology, reminds us, "There is no birth of consciousness without pain." Furthermore, you may expect to encounter beneath the chaos and distress of crisis, an extraordinary individual, uniquely gifted, creative and empowered. And you will recognize that this gifted individual is none other than yourself.

And so, as you begin your journey, we wish you well. Do not forget that one day, when you have completed your quest, you will find, upon your return, others who will seek you out and will ask you what you have learned. Look forward to telling them your tale: the pleasure of that telling is part of your reward.

———————————————

Who gets up early to discover the moment light begins?
Who finds us here circling, bewildered, like atoms?
Who comes to a spring thirsty
and sees the moon reflected in it?
Who, like Jacob blind with grief and age, smells the shirt
of his lost son
and can see again?
Who lets a bucket down and brings up
a flowing prophet? Or like Moses, goes for fire
and finds what burns inside the sunrise?
Jesus slips into a house to escape enemies,
and opens a door to the other world.
Solomon cuts open a fish, and there's a gold ring.
Omar storms in to kill the prophet
and leaves with blessings.
Chase the deer and end up everywhere!
An oyster opens his mouth to swallow one drop.

Now there's a pearl.
A vagrant wanders empty ruins.
Suddenly he's wealthy.
But don't be satisfied with stories, how things
have gone with others.
Unfold your own myth,
without complicated explanation,
so everyone will understand the passage,
We have opened you.

Start walking toward Shams, Your legs will get heavy
and tired. Then comes a moment
of feeling the wings you've grown,
lifting.

RUMI
[from *These Branching Moments, Odes by Rumi,*
translated by John Moyne and Coleman Barks]

1

THE PROBLEM and PROMISE of FAILURE

Life moves on, whether we act as cowards or heroes. Life has no other discipline to impose, if we would but realize it, than to accept life unquestioningly. Everything we shut our eyes to, everything we run away from, everything we deny, denigrate or despise, serves to defeat us in the end. What seems nasty, painful, evil, can become a source of beauty, joy and strength, if faced with an open mind. Every moment is a golden one for him who has the vision to recognize it as such.

HENRY MILLER

Ours is a world where people don't know what they want and are willing to go through hell to get it.

DON MARQUIS

Results! Why, man, I have gotten a lot of results. I know several thousand things that won't work.

THOMAS A. EDISON

WHEN I WAS IN THE MIDDLE of my failure crisis — the story is given in detail in the Appendix; see "The Author's Story" — I scoured the bookshelves for something to read that would lead me out of the doldrums. There wasn't much. That was a few years ago. There isn't much now. This in itself is surprising. Even in my most optimistic moments I suppose I would have admitted that failure of one sort or another was universal, part of everyone's experience. Why were there so few titles? During the years since my own crisis, I have thought long and hard about why this might be so. Today, I would say that, even with the enormous popularity and proliferation of books on psychology (which necessarily deal indirectly with failure of all sorts), the culture was just not ready to look deeply into the mirror. This was the mid- to late 1980s, the Reagan years, when becoming a millionaire was an act of patriotism, no matter what it took to get there. At any rate, I read what books were available, notably Carole Hyatt and Linda Gottlieb's book *When Smart People Fail*. That was helpful to me, and it may be to you as well, although their sample of interviewees tends to be restricted to white collar executives. But in general, the few available titles fall into two categories: one, the endless iteration of success mantras of the "Power of Positive Thinking" school, and, two, the recovery books. Surprisingly, even the recovery books were, for me, unsatisfying.

This seemed strange. After all, wasn't success the normal state of health for any capable, intelligent, optimistic adult in our society? I could see that if I were experiencing failure — which I certainly was, judging from my bank account, my frame of mind and my prospects — then I needed to "take the cure," to get back on my feet and turn things around. But I couldn't get started. Gradually, I began to see that it wasn't "recovery" I was after. The recovery books seemed to imply that with enough hard work and self-discipline, I would be able to restore myself to my previous quality of life. Then (after a long period of doubt) it came to me: that was the last thing I wanted! It was the quality of my previous life that had caused me to fail in the first place. I did not wish to recover from error so that I could be restored to error. I saw eventually and came to feel strongly that there were deeper causes and currents underlying my experience.

I got to the point where it seemed that I really didn't have any other alternative than to begin with what I had, and what I had was *failure*. With no other choice, I adopted what might be called an experimental attitude regarding my own experience. I decided to try to discover what was really going on both within myself and on the outside, and to determine what was actually at stake. It was my hope that by doing so, I could break what seemed like a depressing cycle of defeat I had known year after year.

Time to reflect and to study was one unusual advantage in my favor. I was able to scale down my responsibilities and obligations, and make a space in my life to examine closely what was happening. In this I was very lucky. I owe a lot to my immediate family for their patience. We lived in a house where the rent was not high, in a small town that was relatively inexpensive, and one way or another we were able to keep going. I read widely, retrieved much from earlier studies in college and elsewhere, spent hours in conversation. I looked into everything I could think of to get at the truth of my failure experience.

What I discovered from this lengthy and eclectic search was that failure was not simply a problem. There was — latent within the experience — a potential reward. Understanding that reward — what it is and how we can claim it — depends heavily on how well we have developed a clear understanding of failure itself, in a general sense and in the particulars of our own experience.

DEFINING FAILURE

If you have made mistakes, even serious ones, there is always another chance for you. What we call real failure is not the falling down, but the staying down.

MARY PICKFORD (actress)

"There is no failure if there is growth." — ANNETTE

"That is insane! " — MICHEL

"I have been a failure all my life, and I am in great company. In numerous ways, I am proud of my failures, as they have made me a stronger, more spiritual human being." — JACK

For most of us, coming to some understanding of failure is a catch-as-catch-can affair. Success is another matter. Everyone has a concept of what constitutes success. It may not really be their own; they may have picked it up without thinking from parents or school or peer group. It may be completely inauthentic in terms of their own individuality — based neither in reality or truth — and radically unsuitable. But as long as they hold it, they hold it dear. For most people, failure is merely the space that's left when success has departed. Failure is "that-which-is-not-success."

However, failure is understood quite differently by people who have met failure head-on and reflected on it deeply. Among those we interviewed, some came to see failure as a developmental stage or a temporary but natural condition that eventually yielded some positive result. For others, it was a word that in the long run simply had ceased to be useful, and consequently they had dropped it from their vocabulary. This will certainly be more easily said than done for those suffering in the midst of a very serious failure. But even in the more extreme cases, from the many failure stories we've heard, one thing is mentioned repeatedly: failure, to those who have lived through it, is no longer a valid component of the individual's self-concept.

The point is not to dismiss "failure" as a senseless aberration but to look carefully at its many and often shifting *meanings*.

First of all there is the every-day vernacular meaning. An engine fails. A heart fails. I fail to make a right turn. I fail a test. I fail to remember our anniversary. Now, of course, there may be greater and more troubling failures beneath the surface in any of these cases. The engine may have failed because I failed to be responsible and have the oil checked. My heart may fail if I throw myself into a self-destructive lifestyle. But, in general, the word "failure" has a simple utility that need not be dispensed with. There is, however, another more important way of understanding the term.

Etymologically, the word "failure" comes into English from the Latin word, meaning to deceive or disappoint. (The words "fallacy" and "fallible" derive from the same root.) In many cases, a psychological crisis, and its accompanying anguish and confusion, does not mark the beginning but the end of failure, the point where failure, after existing for whatever length of time unnoticed, becomes manifest. The pain we feel in failure is at the *collapse* of something — an idea or a belief, a definition of ourselves or a relationship we have with others. We held this something to be indispensable to our well-being, but in reality, failure shows it to be partial or limiting or obsolete. Then one of two things may happen. Our former certainty is either made less important relative to beliefs or commitments or it is exposed as the root of our problem and is rejected entirely. In other words, the advent of some new truth — through the experience of *failure* — reveals what had been a deception in one's life.

This book contains many stories about failure and therefore many nuances in the way failure is defined. But here at the outset, let's cast a definition of failure in this way.

Failure is the collapse or deterioration of a concept, belief, commitment or activity to which we had formerly given ourselves with real intensity; *and* it is usually a key part of a developmental process that can, if nurtured well, bring us to see that what was ending (what was "failing") did so because we misunderstood our own changing reality, both interior (psychological or spiritual) and exterior (social, economic, etc.). Failure is not just the absence of success but a force in its own right. It is almost always painful and in this respect it bears an unnerving resemblance to the painfulness of both death and birth. Indeed failure *is* both death and birth and it challenges us to embrace it as such.

Having said this, extreme care should be exercised as one searches for the deceptions and misunderstandings in one's life. This is very, very hard to do, and sometimes impossible without professional assistance, for the questions are myriad and interwoven. Take for example a divorce. Where does the deception of failure lie? Was it self-deception? Or was one partner deceiving the other? Was deception in any of its guises — denial, disingenuousness, evasion — a characteristic of the relationship? Were the individuals set up for failure by deceptiveness and dysfunction in their families of origin? And was there a still greater deception on the outside? A social one that includes and surrounds them in their particular experience? Were they unconsciously conforming to cultural standards or taboos that may have been inconsistent with their true personas? Pinning down the deception at the heart of such a failure is further compounded because in most cases many of these factors — and others besides — may be involved at the same time. The point is that in thinking about failure, we must approach the problem with care, if for no other reason than to avoid closing off possibilities of other interpretations.

BETTER THINGS TO COME

Let's take a look briefly here at what the benefits of failure might be — all of this to be explored in greater depth in subsequent chapters. To use my own failure experience as an example, there is, first of all, the natural benefit that comes from being required to look at something that needed attention. Denial of my long string of failures at that stage for me was no longer an option; things in my work life and home life were too dramatically off-kilter for that. Second, as a result of this specific self-awareness that developed when I stopped denying my failure, I was led to a greater clarity generally. This, in turn, brought me, not without suffering, to greater vitality, spontaneity, and greater self-expression. My sense of meaningful participation in relationships and connection to the world at large increased. In short, a tranformation was beginning to take place. Without my experience of failure, this may never have occurred. Later, while writing this book, I discovered that this process of growth through failure was more common than I might have suspected.

Time after time, the individuals I spoke with told stories of hardship and crisis that turned out — in retrospect — not to have been failures at all. That is, not ultimately failures. The challenge, therefore, is how did they and how did I *get to* "the retrospect"? The answer invariably involved some fundamental change in behavior or attitude or perception. So it's this elusive and deeply personalized transformation that we're after. Not mere "recovery" in the usual sense, but "discovery," a word that conjures up images of a journey of exploration — like Columbus discovering the New World. (Another notable failure, by the way: he was, after all, looking for India.)

In a letter dated 1906, psychologist William James wrote

> *Most people live, whether physically, intellectually or morally, in a very restricted circle of their potential being. They make use of a very small portion of their possible consciousness, and their soul's resources in general, much like a man who, out of his whole bodily organism, should get into a habit of using and moving only his little finger. Great emergencies and crises show us how much greater our vital resources are than we had supposed.* [1]

Submission and defeat at the hands of failure can imprison us in the tightest of all "restricted circles." Mesmerized by our misfortunes, pursuing distractions that pull our attention away from the real situation, blaming oneself or others, nothing moves forward; nothing changes. Our sentence drags on wearily. The good news is that by accepting the challenge of the failure experience we can break through such restraints into a life that is rich and abundant.

It is the promise that inheres in those "vital resources" referred to by James that makes it possible to remain stubbornly optimistic even in the worst of circumstances. The discovery that there is more — much more — outside the circle of our own limited experience than had ever been imagined is both the means by which self-transformation occurs and the direction toward which it tends.

EXPERIENCE YOUR EXPERIENCE

Listen to our interviewees as they reflect on their positive gains from failure:

"This experience was severe, very destructive, and in many ways harmed me. But I don't regret it. It means I have experienced the depths, and I value that greatly." — ANNE

"If I could do it all over again, have all that not happen? I don't know that I would want that. Partly because it's the only life I've known, and partly because I think there's something about living a very different life that seems special. You see a different dimension of humanness. You see into deeper recesses of what human experience holds, and there's something about that breadth of experience which is enriching. I don't regret that." — CHRISTINE

"Without failure, there can be no knowing. There is no information to be had unless you have both positive and negative information. Without negative information, you know nothing." — BERT

What does it take for the process of transformation to occur? First and last, and every step along the way, the answer is the same: "Experience Your Experience." Nothing can proceed, nothing healthy can even make a start, until an individual agrees to encounter life without evasion or denial. Nothing could be simpler or harder to do. First of all, one may very well encounter resistance. Society is ambivalent about how many fully alert people it wants running around. If you don't believe me, try going to a party and talking about something that matters. People will quickly drift away. Furthermore, by the time we reach adulthood, the routines and habits of daily life begin to solidify around us so that experiencing anything — different or differently — is difficult because so little that is genuinely novel is permitted to enter the scope of our vision. We become, in a sense, psychologically and spiritually, near-sighted and seeing little at that. Moreover, contemporary culture, with its fast-paced electronic media as a basis, would have us believe that all problems are fixable, fast. Our attention span — even for our own troubles — shrinks. But failure will not be hurried and normally requires that we remain in the failure experience for a good long time.

When failure happens, one is faced with an anomaly. The experience doesn't make sense, it doesn't fit with one's understanding of the world. Because of this, the temptation to deny it or explain it away can be almost irresistible. However, those we spoke with who were able more fully to encounter the reality of their experience, who let failure have the time it needed, developed an ability to see in these anomalies important opportunities for growth. For many it wasn't easy to get to that point. It took a first-rate failure, one that could not be overlooked or repackaged into "a blessing in disguise" or "a cloud with a silver lining," and then it took real courage to go into the experience, stay there long enough for truly new insights to develop and only then receive whatever value they could find.

JUDGMENT

The greatest discovery of my generation is that a human being can alter his life by altering his attitudes of mind.

WILLIAM JAMES

Since nothing we intend is ever faultless, and nothing we attempt ever without error, and nothing we achieve without some measure of finitude and fallibility we call humanness, we are saved by forgiveness.

DAVID AUGSBURGER

As a picture of the failure phenomenon starts to emerge, and as we begin to make out the various features and aspects of the experience, it becomes easier for us to see what it is we are dealing with. Failure enters the picture all dressed up as a problem but carries in its inside pockets the promise of change. This change can have about it the quality of transformation, because it is more than a mere altering or shifting between related pieces. Instead, it represents for the individual the formation of a new constellation around a different and more personally relevant organizing center, or as Joseph Campbell describes it: "a shift in the axis mundi."

In order to achieve a new synthesis, a new viewpoint about failure, we must embark on a journey. Along the way we will encounter experiences that may be fearful and mysterious. Nevertheless, we must encounter them in their full reality without evasion or the interposing of artificial distance.

In this encounter there will be temptations. One subtle and powerful temptation will arise from the reflex to assess whatever we observe and place it within some already existing framework.

For example, when an individual tells himself he is a failure, a judgment has been made. This act of judgment is significant. Why did the individual choose the word "failure"— a word which has all the gravity and sense of finality of a jury verdict? Why not a more moderate expression such as "setback" or "disappointment" or "problem?" By whose standard is the assessment of "failure" made? Was there something inherent in the experience that made this judgment unequivocal? What about the system of values and set of beliefs by which the person lives? Does it not allow for some other interpretation of that which is being judged a failure? If not, why not? Many people who are in the midst of a failure miss the opportunity to ask these entirely legitimate questions.

Failure, therefore, often is turned into a judgment that people pass upon their experience or, worse, on themselves. How dangerous this is, and yet how hard to resist! For when individuals feel that some action of their own has brought on their failure crisis, eliminated their options, and removed all possibility for constructive engagement with life, they may begin to define themselves accordingly. Such automatic inner-directed criticism is just as dangerous as is automatic blaming of other people for one's own mistakes. But in the last analysis, it is not their experience but their judgment on their experience which brings this harshness to pass.

However, here, as always, judgment must be bounded by prudence. It is wiser not to judge — not yet — and not precipitously. As we gaze into the face of this failure experience, we may make an astonishing discovery. Here is not the Medusa, who will turn us into stone if our eyes meet. Here, instead, is mere deception — that like the Incubus — takes flight once we have given it its name. Or, here is the phoenix, that magical bird with the wisdom to know that by accepting a fiery death in the present, it will rise resplendently from the ashes in the future.

After this climactic struggle, which occurs in the darkest regions of our journey, we are rewarded for our courage with a new gift of self-understanding. We find we have arrived at that point (the "retrospect") where we can say along with so many of the people you will hear from in this book: "Now I see that it was no failure after all."

Beyond this matter of inner development — outside our immediate frame of reference — there is a larger arena, where the struggle to understand failure and success also takes place. This arena is the *society* in which we live. It is to this that we now will turn.

2

FAILURE and SOCIETY
Values, Causes, Meanings

More than any time in history mankind faces a crossroads. One path leads to despair and utter hopelessness, the other to total extinction. Let us pray that we have the wisdom to choose correctly.

WOODY ALLEN

We have an economic system which can only function by expanding, and when it stops expanding it collapses. It has no stability. The only stability it has is growth. Now, if you have a world that is finite and you unleash an economic force that can only survive by growing, one day the irresistible force is going to reach the immovable object. That's happening. So, globally, at the highest level of generalization we're already beginning to feel the limits. And on top of that our industrial push has created the environmental crisis. I mean that is why we have an environmental crisis. Because of absolutely uncritical decisions and the inability — which may be intrinsic to the human — to predict consequences. But it is a classic American thing to say: "Hey, look at this, it's gasoline. See, it explodes. It's a source of power. We ought to use it and make a vehicle run on it." Yes, a vehicle. One vehicle. But 72 million vehicles? What happened to the

33

multiplier effect of our technological innovations? Nobody thinks about that. So you've created the environmental crisis. Now when people go to resort areas in the Adirondacks they are depressed, because they literally can see the effects of the economic system — that they are benefiting from — on the world as it is, on nature. They see dead lakes. And trees with no leaves on them. I mean it's dead. Dead. And that is a very shocking thing. That will give you a sense of malaise. That's why when the surgical needles wash up on the beach, everybody goes berserk. Because something is definitely, self-evidently, out of whack. We have always thought of ourselves as the wilderness nation, as having unlimited resources. Now we realize the system is closed.

STEPHEN MARINI
Professor, Wellesley College

ONE OF THE MOST COMMON OPINIONS we received from the individuals we interviewed in all parts of the country — was that social failure is becoming more and more a part of our contemporary experience. The reasons for this are complex. Some have to do with the shrinking size of the world and the fact that there are fewer places to bury our mistakes. Failures that once we were able to keep secret, are now the subject of the evening news. Examples abound; three big ones have been Three Mile Island, Bhopal, Chernobyl. The complexity of nearly everyone's life is increasing. Things are not going that well. A family that could exist on one salary a generation ago, with security and leisure time, now comes up short. Now both spouses must work, and, even so, have little or no time to enjoy the fruits of their efforts. Socially, our problems are maddeningly intransigent. From homelessness and the increasing violence in our cities to the crisis in our financial institutions, and the colossal federal and state deficits, our problems don't go away, they just take turns capturing the public attention. Globally, we are reaching the outer limits of success as we have understood it, and the evidence of a possible systemic social failure is appearing on the horizon.

Why should we look at society as we try to understand the problem of *personal* failure? The answer lies in the special context that society provides for individuals who in their unique circumstances are working out the issues of failure and success. A society is many things. It is a repository for tradition. A maintainer of systems of belief. An organization that provides for the security of its constituents. It is also a context where individuals make sense of things. If I am feeling lost and am groping for direction, I may turn to my society and receive the orientation that I need. Through my interactions with my peers and by a process of checking my life against conventional standards, I can gauge where I am and where I am going. But nowadays there are changes that are specific to our time in history. Although the experience of those who preceded us is analogous, and the ways in which people deal with failure may be similar, there is no getting away from the fact that today we are up against ultimate environmental limits that call us to respond decisively and in ways that may depart from tradition. These limits — set by nuclear arsenals and the deteriorating environment — have existed for decades as theoretical considerations, but now they are actual and present, impinging on the conditions of modern life. This is new. This has not happened before.

Within these social and cultural limits — which, from a historical perspective have only recently become relevant — the struggle for meaning in personal life continues as a perennial theme. One of our respondents spoke of a conversation with his father, a man who had achieved great success from relatively humble beginnings. The son had had persistent difficulties in finding himself, in feeling at home in contemporary society, and in settling down to a career. His explanation was that nothing he had tried struck him as personally relevant, meaningful or worthwhile. The father was mystified. He did not understand how his son's personal, psychological concerns were relevant. Surely the purpose in life was to work hard at some respectable activity and achieve financial independence and the recognition of one's peers. What more could there be to it than that? His assessment of the question of meaningfulness was that it was a sort of spiritual distemper contracted by those who know they do not have to work for mere survival. Whether the father or the son is more "correct" in his opinion, is not the issue. What is inescapable, however, is that the question of personal meaningfulness in everyday life is a real question, one that does not go away (unless repressed), and for which an answer must be sought. In this case, the son went into the human services and has thrived in his newfound vocation. The point of the story is that one must take what one has — even if it includes questions that seem irrelevant and troublesome to others — and begin there. The point is not to get saddled with a set of expectations imposed from without, or to become disoriented personally by the apparent aimlessness and entropy in contemporary social, cultural, political, and economic life. This is a tall order for many people whose personal failures seem to be, and often are, grounded in society's, or a large institution's, failure to function smoothly.

Failure, therefore, is a global, societal, and personal phenomenon. Faced with this fact, we have to decide not merely what we think we ought to do with the results of personal failure, but also we have to decide what we think and feel about failure in our society itself. This chapter is an attempt to see the failure phenomenon both personally and in the wider social context in which it frequently occurs. Societal failure is a phenomenon which, in fact, is a curious mixture of good news and bad news and which — although it may feel like Death itself — is nothing other than Life turned with its back to us.

JIM'S STORY

Fit, and handsome in an outdoorsman's craggy way, and topped by a mop of snow-white hair, Jim is reminiscent of the mountains he loves to ski on. Past the usual age of retirement, his life has grown even more full and interesting. He tells a story in which his loss of a sense of self precipitated a serious depression just as he was approaching what seemed like a career coup. It was a missed opportunity to perform well in the outer (business) world that had failure written all over it. Yet his downfall had the promise of a new wholeness in it as well. The only catch was, getting there took him years.

"I grew up in a smallish town, the son of a local shopkeeper. I didn't have too much in common with my parents — my dad was interested in the outdoors and physical activity. I was quite introverted, sedentary and bookish. They were content with their lives. I was restless — I couldn't wait to move out and broaden my horizons. I had great aspirations for my life.

"Ever since I was in high school, I had had a very clear perception of what it would mean to be successful. I had read Fred Wakeman's *The Hucksters* [1946], a romantic exposé of the advertising profession. Later, it was made into a film with Clark Gable, Deborah Kerr and Sydney Greenstreet [MGM, 1947]. In this story, advertising was clearly a swinging business with fascinating, glib-tongued people who were into romance and each other's pants, and there was conniving and lots of glamor. I thought, 'That's for me!' and I became enamored of the idea of being an account executive for a large ad agency.

"After 3½ years serving in World War II, my upwardly mobile aspirations were satisfied by getting into an Ivy League college. I think I was the only person being rushed for a fraternity who had gone to a public high school.

"I kept my eye on my career goal, and after graduation landed a job 'in marketing and advertising,' peddling Vicks VapoRub through small towns in the South. This was a coveted job at the time, very good for the resume, and so I was thrilled to get it. I was actually a 'drummer,' a person who drums up sales by beating the bushes in the hinterlands. I would drive from town to town in my 1947 Ford, which was stuffed with boxes of Vicks VapoRub, advertising materials, an industrial-strength stapler, and a ladder. I peddled the boxes of product to general stores — that was the 'marketing' part. I used the ladder and stapler to plaster signs all over local barns — that was the 'advertising' part. Then, in the evenings, I got to do 'product research.' In those days, they used to have commercials between shows at the cinemas. My job was to survey the patrons as they left the theater, collecting their impressions of the Vicks VapoRub commercial. Periodically, I'd get stuck in the dry creek beds I was driving along, and the local farmers would have to hitch their mules to the Ford to get me out of the muck and on my way again. I was pretty far from Manhattan's elegant Madison Avenue, but I believed I was making my start in the exotic ad biz.

"Eventually, I moved into a position as advertising manager for a midsized manufacturer. I married, started a family, built a home in suburbia, and was comfortably off and feeling pretty good about my career so far. One day, I had a visit from a salesperson, who happened to mention that a large ad agency in town was looking for a guy in the media department. 'Why don't you go in and talk?' I interviewed for the position of assistant to the media director. Although I was offered the job, I turned it down because it wasn't glamorous enough. It was all about numbers, circulation, statistics . . . not at all creative. Later, they called back and told me that their top account executive was retiring, would I like to take his place? Would I!?! I was given a tremendous send-off by my former firm, took this dream job, and that's when I fell flat on my face.

"I decided that if I was going to succeed at this once-in-a-lifetime job, I had to be the epitome of the swinging, savvy, all-knowing ad man. I felt that this was my chance to prove that I really was Clark Gable in *The Hucksters*. I thought I was expected to know everything about everything in 24 hours, that I had to be in high key all the time, that I had to be a glib, sophisticated star. Well, of course I wasn't that kind of person at all. The reason I had done as well as I had was that although I'm very creative, I'm also a rational, dependable, solid person — kind of a straight arrow. But I didn't want to be that — I wanted to be flamboyant!

"The self-imposed pressure quickly mounted. I began to lose sleep. I would go to bed and be in a delirium — not really asleep or awake — and in the morning I'd be exhausted. I became paranoid — I was sure people were looking at me funny, sizing me up. I was married at that time to a woman who was a hypochondriac and suicidal. She was constantly putting me down — and so I doubted my abilities even more. For the first time in my life, I absolutely lost my self-esteem. Soon, I considered myself a cipher, totally inept, not up to the job. Eventually, I confided to my boss that I didn't think I was cutting it and he couldn't understand why I felt concerned. That didn't help — I kept losing sleep until I was getting the shakes. I felt like a fraud. Finally, after six months, I quit the job and took a nosedive into a nervous breakdown.

"The antidote to depression in those days — the late '50s — was amphetamines. They were popular among overweight women, and I had no trouble getting my hands on a good supply. For $13.00 I could buy a pint of the little capsules. I thought they were terrific! They made me feel creative, uninhibited, like the king of the world! I took a job selling insurance; I never really made any money at it and spent my days drinking coffee at a local pastry shop. At this point, I still had a wife, three kids, and a mortgage, and absolutely no trust in my abilities. I was floundering, looking for answers. I happened to pick up a copy of *Advertising Age*, and noticed an ad in the Help Wanted section for someone to do sales promotion for a nationally circulated magazine, based in a rural area. The sales promotion part attracted my professional interest, but the idea of living in the country really grabbed me — I was ready to get out of suburbia. I went out for the job interview, still high on amphetamines, made a dynamic presentation and won the position.

"My family happily moved to a small town in the hills of New England, intrigued by the promise of a big farmhouse, a horse, a dog, and a happier father. I was still trying to get my bearings after failing so miserably as an advertising executive and as an insurance salesman, and was shocked when the local doctor refused to prescribe more amphetamines. So it was a complete, unintended withdrawal, which was really tough after a couple of years on the stuff.

"After a few false starts with various jobs and some slow recuperation, I found myself working as a 'one-man-show,' director of creative programs and special projects for a major division of a large corporation. I had finally figured out that my old dream job — of being an advertising account executive — basically meant being a mail carrier between the client and the agency's creative department. So I was happy with this opportunity to work in-house, and I was there for almost 25 years. I healed while I was there. Part of that healing was the simple security I felt in being a member of a large corporation. Part of it was that I found myself the only creative thinker in an organization full of scientists, and my creativity was considered to be unusual and highly valuable to the company. I was given free rein to implement my ideas as long as they helped to market our products. The possibilities were almost limitless. Slowly I reemerged from the depths of my nervous breakdown. As I accomplished good things in my job and was recognized for them, I would be drawn out further. It wasn't miraculous, and it wasn't immediate — it was a very gradual rediscovery of self-esteem, to the point where I ultimately was able to recognize and enjoy the fact that I had something valuable and unique to offer.

"I became more daring as I regained my sense of self. Eventually, I was in a position to mold opinion and blaze a whole new trail. I did things that nobody else in the operation had tried, and had some truly exciting successes. I did a lot of traveling in the U.S. and overseas, and I got to meet a lot of interesting people. One of these people was a woman who worked with a film company I had hired for a special project, and she became my second wife.

"I think one of the reasons that I had such a positive experience with this job is that time was on my side. By the time I got this job, I had matured enough to realize that if I kept my mouth shut and listened, and made my move when I was ready, I could accomplish more. I'm convinced that people who have problems can resolve them simply by living day to day and letting time do its work. During that process of time marching on, your senses become keener, your powers of observing yourself and the world around you become greater, and that's part of the maturing process. When I was in the depths of my crisis, I was forced to live day by day. I had three kids to support and that kind of kept me going.

"When I look back on that time in my life, it's still a very poignant feeling for me because I was so shattered by what I considered to be a failure. But if it hadn't happened, I wouldn't be here now. I wouldn't live in this wonderful part of the world, I wouldn't have met my wife, and I wouldn't have the extended family she brought to the marriage.

"You know, when you have an experience like this you lose your identity, and it's as if you lost the person you thought you were and you'll never get him back. Well, I got a more assured person back — a different person that I am much happier with. It was a good experience. I'm 67, and I feel 35. I have such a rich life. I'm still doing consulting work for my last employer, but I'm doing lots of other things. I have a broad network of wonderful friends, whom I enjoy. I am a hiking guide for a health club, and I'm teaching downhill skiing to beginners. Now that's been a wonderful experience, and it proves a point about what we've been talking about: These fledgling skiers are all terrified of putting those long slats on their big, heavy boots and heading down that steep mountain, and they keep apologizing when they fall. And I just reassure them, 'I've been in that spot myself. You're supposed to fall down. That's how you learn.'"

It's hard, sometimes devilishly hard, to see, at say age 25 or 35, what a man (or woman) of 67 can show you about how to live gracefully in the world. In the conspicuous absence of a guiding mentor, Jim struggled for many years to find his own way. For a long time he was lost in a forest of apparent failures that seemed, and were, intensely personal. But hindsight showed him something we can all benefit from remembering: that personal identity (including goals and aspirations such as becoming a high-flying advertising account executive) consists not only of whatever we are by ourselves on the inside, our basic character and personality, but also of what we take in or graft onto ourselves from the outside, from the not-necessarily-healthy world of social and cultural values. Jim swallowed hook, line, and sinker an idea of himself playing a businessman's role for which he was not suited. His failure was not just his own but society's too: nothing in his schooling, military service, or early years of employment helped him separate illusion from reality in determining who and what he wanted to — and really could — become. His problems with failure were compounded by other influences from the outside — a wife who needed help herself and a medical establishment with values that justified throwing drugs at the symptoms of Jim's failure rather than prescribing other means to get at the causes. It can even be said that the cultural stereotypes Jim mistakenly took seriously (the "successful" advertising executives in *The Hucksters*) were for him, as they are for all of us, examples of what students of mythology like Joseph Campbell and Robert Bly[1] call "defective mythology." These characters seem exciting at first glance but turn out to be only two-dimensional with no real depth. They do not truly know themselves; their lives are inauthentic. If we take them as our models, as our compass for finding a way through our own self-development, we cannot help but be misled.

Who owns the failures in Jim's story? He tells his tale without recriminations against others and with a redeeming sense of humor about himself. But the responsibility for the predicament his failure and breakdown represented lay as much with the society in which he lives as with himself. His evolution toward peace of mind and fulfillment reminds us of William James' observation, quoted above, that "the greatest discovery of my generation is that a human being can alter his life by altering his attitudes of mind."

OUR CULTURAL MYTHOLOGY

Americans love heroes. Characters arise from our national ethos and stride into posterity: John Wayne at the Alamo, Gary Cooper at High Noon, or Bogart's Rick Blaine brooding over a bottle in Casablanca. The names and faces change but the great American archetype is perennial: the tough, self-reliant, independent outsider who knows what's right, does what's right and asks no reward. But in our culture, our love for heroes, just like our love for a great many other things, passes over from reverent love into hungry consumption: we consume our heroes, like sandwiches. Responding to this demand, whole industries have grown up that excite and stimulate that desire and then keep it glutted with "product": *Rambo* 1, 2, 3, etc., *ad nauseam*. As Jim's story relates, one of the most venerable and conspicuous and seductive of these industries is Hollywood. In recent years, the distinction between filmmaking and advertising has deteriorated to the point where some of our heroes now begin life not as the work of screenwriters but of toymakers. Now, instead of the heroes we need — and need desperately — who can inspire us to take on the challenges facing us as a culture and a nation, what do we have? Worse yet, what do our impressionable children have? Pizza-eating turtles.

It is difficult to escape the effects of these cultural influences. We are surrounded constantly by messages from promoters of one or another of these cultural archetypes or artifacts. They seek to persuade us to accept — or, at least, not to object to — the content behind these messages, content which is often violent, sexist, and racist. Beyond this threat, however, there is another danger which receives less attention: the danger that through habitual participation in a defective cultural mythology, we begin to lose our own identities. When this happens, we suffer. One way or another, sooner or later, we come to grief. This is what Jim's story illustrates so clearly. Having achieved an apotheosis of his particular cultural hero, "the ad man," Jim was thrown into catastrophe. There is a sense of inevitability that one feels in reading his story that arises from his failure carefully to examine himself and the direction of his life and his uncritical, un-self-reflective adoption of a Hollywood myth. The good news in Jim's story lies at the heart of his failure experience precisely at that point where his integrity and inauthenticity collide.

Myths have an attractive force. They are centripetal. We are "taken in," and we refashion our personal, private world to suit our new identity. This adaptation is not necessarily bad. Who hasn't taken on the role of a favorite hero as a guide in times of crisis? A tennis player, for example, who late in the match finds herself down a set, might very well imagine that she is Martina Navratilova, determined and strong, seizing victory at the moment when defeat seemed all but assured. Congruencies — real or imagined — between a heroic model and ourselves can be intensely empowering. It is at particular points of incongruence, however when we may inauthentically alter ourselves to fit an inappropriate or defective model — that trouble may begin, and, because no model can fit anyone of us perfectly, all are problematical. Such a bad "fit," such inauthenticity, is a common breeding ground for failure.

Robert N. Bellah, in his well-known book *Habits of the Heart*, discusses a centrally important and beloved myth that lies at the very heart of our American identity, the cowboy hero. However, even this archetype becomes problematical. Fun to believe in, tough to live by: a setup for failure if taken literally as a guide.

A deep and continuing theme in American literature is the hero who must leave society, alone or with a few others, in order to realize the moral good in the wilderness, at sea, or on the margins of settled society. Sometimes the withdrawal involves a contribution to society, as in James Fenimore Cooper's The Deerslayer. *Sometimes the new marginal community realizes its ethical ends are impossible in the larger society, as in the interracial harmony between Huckleberry Finn and [the black slave] Jim. Sometimes the flight from society is simply mad and ends in general disaster, as in* Moby Dick. *When it is not in and through society but in flight from it that the good is to be realized, as in the case of Melville's Ahab, the line between ethical heroism and madness vanishes, and the destructive potentiality of a completely asocial individualism is revealed.*

America is also the inventor of that most mythic individual hero, the cowboy, who again and again saves the society he can never completely fit into. The cowboy has a special talent — he can shoot straighter and faster than other men — and a special sense of justice. But these characteristics make him so unique that he can never fully belong to society. His destiny is to defend society without ever really joining it. He rides off alone into the sunset like Shane, or, like the Lone Ranger, moves on accompanied only by his Indian companion. But the cowboy's importance is not that he is isolated or antisocial. Rather, his significance lies in his unique, individual virtue and special skills and it is because of those qualities that society needs and welcomes him. Shane, after all, starts as a real outsider, but ends up with the gratitude of the community and the love of a woman and a boy. And while the Lone Ranger never settles down and marries the local schoolteacher, he always leaves with the affection and gratitude of the people he has helped. It is as if the myth says you can be a truly good person, worthy of admiration and love, only if you resist fully joining the group. But sometimes the tension leads to an irreparable break. The hero of High Noon, *Will Kane, abandoned by the cowardly townspeople, saves them from an unrestrained killer, but then throws his sheriff's badge in the dust and goes off into the desert with his bride. One is left wondering where they will go, for there is no longer any link with the town.*[2]

For over two hundred years we have lived securely with our cultural myths, like the cowboy-hero, intact: we are the prodigies of history. Nothing lies outside our reach. With our unlimited resources — physical, intellectual, economic, artistic — we are a nation bursting with creative genius. Americans are history's greatest optimists. As a nation we have maintained a perennial belief in the irresistible power of our cheerfulness, our idealism, our democratic vision, and our ability to "make it happen."

In their book, *The Predicament of the Prosperous*, authors Bruce Birch and Larry Rasmussen, refer to "the cluster of assumptions" that have shaped the American vision. In general these assumptions apply to five areas:

1. Our understanding and use of the environment
2. Our faith in materialism

3. Our commitment to economic and technological
   systems and solutions
4. Our belief in the unlimited human potential for good
5. Our faith in the individual and social rewards of
   competitiveness, education and hard work.[3]

It should not come as news to anyone that these assumptions have in recent years become qualified (at least) by a growing awareness of the world which has to absorb the impact of our actions. Environmentalists who warn of the threat to our ecosystem are no longer dismissed as cranks. The materialism so fashionable in the 1970s and '80s is vulgar in the '90s. Classical Marxism (in collapse) and classical capitalism (run amok) are both in disrepute. Technological prowess has been replaced by technological menace. Humans continue to exhibit a potential for evil, and competitiveness, hard work and education cannot guarantee a thing. What then of our heroes to whom we look for guidance? While some people turn to gurus who have answers for every question, many more people grapple with failure — and success — in their personal lives without the clear reference points that a coherent, clear-thinking society can offer. It's no wonder people feel lost.

On a global basis, our industrial society is facing failure of an unprecedented magnitude. At the World Assembly on Justice, Peace and the Integrity of Creation held recently in Seoul, the following statistics were offered:

Every minute the countries of the world spend 1.8 million US dollars on military equipment.

Every hour 1500 children die of hunger or of diseases caused by hunger.

Every day a plant or animal species becomes extinct.

In the 1980s, every week more people were arrested, tortured, put to flight or oppressed in other ways by repressive governments than at any other time in history.

Every month, through the international economy, a further 7.5 billion US dollars are added to the 1500-

billion dollar debt which has already put an intolerable burden on people in the Third World.

Every year, the rain forest is irretrievably decimated by a surface area corresponding to two-thirds of Korea.

Every decade, the temperature of the earth's atmosphere will rise drastically (by 1.5 to 4.5 degrees Celsius by the middle of the next century), raising the sea level, if the present global warming continues. This will have devastating effects, above all on the coastal areas of all continents.[4]

At this time in our history and in the history of the world, we are faced with the need to make difficult changes in the way we see ourselves and our relationship to others. As a culture we are beset on all sides by the deterioration of many of those beliefs upon which we created the infrastructure of our society. These beliefs have remained for the most part hidden under the surface of our daily activities, which themselves acquired meaning only through their relationship to what lay below. This is the characteristic of basic assumptions: because they are assumed, they do not require much attention; we can take them for granted. It is only when circumstances change — when things that make no sense according to the old order begin to multiply in our experience — that it becomes critical to bring our fundamental beliefs out of the shadows to study them in the light of day.

Our society's disengagement with its own once widely-held central beliefs has left many men and women in limbo. Apparent personal failures multiply when societal failure increases. But many individuals misread their personal failures and ignore the external, societal component within them, thus compounding their private problems by heaping blame solely on themselves. Peripheral vision — of the world-at-large — is a valuable tool.

While it is clear that much of our traditional mythology is obsolete, it is not yet clear where our new myths and our new reality will come from. One thing does seem clear: a new way of envisioning the world and the way each one of us defines our relationship to it will have to emerge from somewhere. If the old notions of success cease to help us, then perhaps the current experience of failure is where we need to look. Our responses to the failures around us will help to shape our new identity first as individuals and then, perhaps, as a world community.

A (VERY) SHORT HISTORY OF THE IDEA OF SUCCESS IN AMERICA

To understand how we have arrived at our contemporary North American misunderstanding of success and failure, it is helpful to go right back to the beginning — right back to Plymouth Rock. The Pilgrims who landed there were members of the separatist English Puritan movement that had developed out of the turmoil of the European Reformation. Setting off from the Netherlands (where they had failed to find acceptance) on the Mayflower, they were 101 religious refugees looking for a place to settle where they might be free of persecution. Their intended destination was the Virginia Colony, which they missed by several hundred miles — landing on the inhospitable coast of Massachusetts at Plymouth on December 21, 1620.

Strongly Calvinistic, the Pilgrims asserted both the unequivocal authority of the Bible and the depravity of the human person. Only through faith did one have any chance of redemption, and in this life one could never know for certain whether or not one was saved. As John Bunyan's classic *Pilgrim's Progress* (1678) makes excruciatingly clear, life for a Puritan was a daily trial, with the fires of Hell on one side and the faint hope of safety — which one dared not presume — on the other.

However, even though a Puritan could not know one's fate for certain, one could look for clues. When something went well, or when one encountered success, it was just possible that this was a sign of Grace, of divine favor. On the contrary, when things went badly, one could pretty well assume the worst. With a theology like this, the Pilgrims' first winter in the New World must have been jolly indeed. Half their party was cut down by disease, and the new colony scarcely made it through to the next harvest — and might not have done so without the help of their Native American neighbors. But they did make it. And so, what were they to conclude? Again, according to their religious beliefs, the survival of the remnant community just possibly might be a sign of Grace for the individuals within it. As the years went by and the little colony persevered, they might well have dared to hope that this was an indication of God's continuing favor, and when they began not merely to survive but to prosper, so much more so.

Another element of the Calvinist religious teaching, which figures in the early history of the idea of success in America, was the idea that the role one adopts in life — whether at work or at home — is a vocation, a genuine religious calling. If you succeed at your vocation, in other words if you are rewarded financially for the work that you do, then this might be interpreted as God's Grace. Wealth came to be seen as a confirmation of the moral legitimacy of one's activities and a blessing from on high. Also important to the proper fulfillment of one's calling was the performance of good works. An individual had a responsibility to put the rewards of his or her vocation to work for the common good of the community through acts of charity. Indeed, such acts of charity came to be seen as outward signs of inner righteousness.

With the passage of time, the Puritan religious framework that surrounded and to some extent contained this dynamic of Grace and reward in several of the northeastern colonies began to fall away. The ever-seductive and ever-receding frontier, with its less structured social order, drew dissidents of all kinds away from the stricter religious communities near the New England coast. By the end of the 18th century, the dominance of Puritanism was offset by the religious makeup of the new nation, which was considerably diverse (with many denominations of Protestants, a few colonies heavily dominated by Catholics, and a notable presence of Jews in some communities). What's more, the ideological stew had been richly seasoned in the late 18th century by the importation to America of European Enlightenment ideas: the writings of Locke, Montesquieu, Rousseau, and others. The idea of success we see played out in the lives of such founding fathers as Benjamin Franklin and Thomas Jefferson puts a heavy emphasis on the notion that success is the natural reward for hard work and self-discipline. Although in part this view echoes the positive qualities of early Puritanism, these Enlightenment thinkers worked hard not so much to win the favor of a wrathful God but to solidify their own position on earth. These late 18th-century American philosophers laid the groundwork for what was to become the social philosophy America is best known for: pragmatism. Societal role models like Franklin and Jefferson were inventors and creators, unafraid to fail, undaunted by setbacks. Classical liberalism in America came to believe that the human being and society were perfectible. It was only a matter of effort and practice before social and personal failure would be eliminated. This spirit of self-confidence and cultural confidence expanded further as the western frontier opened in the 19th century. The optimists — such as Emerson and Whitman at mid-century, to cite literary men who spoke for the culture as a whole — saw no reason to acknowledge failure at all: success was out there waiting for any red-blooded man or woman who wanted it. The pessimists — Mark Twain, Herman Melville, Theodore Dreiser and W. D. Howells, to name a few — all called into serious question the notion that an individual's failure might be merely his own fault or that he ought to be able to recover *tout de suite*. Obviously the cataclysm of the Civil War and the shame of both black slavery and the genocide carried out against

Native Americans (both in the name of economic progress by and for the superior white race) cast a pall over American self-respect.

In the latter half of the 19th century there emerged a new viewpoint about success and failure: Social Darwinism. In the Calvinism of the colonial era, wealth was seen as a sign of God's favor, but the bestowing of this favor placed upon the individual a responsibility to make some return in goods or services to the community. Not so with Social Darwinism. This was "survival of the fittest" applied to the fields of sociology, economics, and human relations. Now success was seen as an indication of evolutionary superiority: one was entitled to whatever one could acquire — by whatever means — simply by virtue of the ability to do so. And, if in your progress toward whatever it might be that you desire, others go down before you, that must be due to their lower status on the evolutionary ladder. The prey does not question the predator. The robber barons of the Gilded Age were the preeminent examples of Social Darwinism in the flesh and in full swing. Their ruthless acquisition of enormous wealth and power created both demons and heroes in the popular American mind: some segments of the population feared such self-aggrandizing entrepreneurs, while others admired them and dreamed of walking in their shoes. Today's society acts with similar ambivalence toward the likes of Donald Trump, the multi-millionaire real estate developer and casino owner: is he the best America can produce or the worst? A colossal success or a pathetic failure?

The culture of the early 20th century had already established the dynamic of conflicting values, related to definitions of success and failure that we have lived with ever since. The Horatio Alger novels taught us what we already knew: that an American fellow could rise from rags to riches by dint of his own luck and pluck. But getting to the top of the financial pyramid never quite seemed to bring the contentment it was supposed to provide. Serious novels like Fitzgerald's *The Great Gatsby* and films like *The Man in the*

Grey Flannel Suit, though written decades apart, told us the same tale: that failure is often inextricably mixed up with success because this culture makes it hard for us to decide what we really want. It is no mistake that two of the great artists of 20th-century America, both filmmakers and both actors — Charlie Chaplin and Woody Allen — achieved their fame by making of themselves hapless characters whose hard work and good intentions (the very things our forefathers taught us *would* pay off) regularly come to naught. The later 20th century in America has been, simply, confused about how to define success and failure and whether to give more credence to what's in a person's heart or to what's in his or her bank account.

Today, strands of all these traditions remain with us. If you want to justify the pursuit of wealth, you can appeal to the authority of certain contemporary religious figures who — as part of their television ministries — offer viewers instruction on how to manage assets for maximum capital appreciation. Or you can follow the exploits of one or another of our celebrated plutocrats who move in a world so far-removed from most of us that it appears to be almost a higher order of existence, a different evolutionary level. And certainly, a government that assumes it has some kind of obligation to create millionaires, and removes restraints that might get in the way, is acting in a manner that is consistent with the gospel of Social Darwinism: more means better. As the culture becomes more secularized, the acquisition of wealth is elevated to a new status — one with few external references or constraints. It has become an end in itself. But not a satisfying end. The ubiquitous materialism to which it leads is problematical.

On a recent flight from Boston to Pittsburgh, I was leafing though the inflight magazine and ran across an article entitled "Marital Materialism." In discussing the effects of wealth on the quality of relationships, the author, Dr. Bruce Baldwin, uses terms from contemporary psychology I had not encountered before: "materialistic dependency" and "acquisition compulsion."

A materialistic orientation becomes serious when men and women begin to use possessions to define self-esteem and a sense of personal adequacy. Materialistic dependency can be defined as a state of ongoing emotional vulnerability that exists when self-esteem becomes excessively linked to status-oriented possessions. The man or woman who has become materialistically dependent has crossed a line from enjoying the possessions to emotionally needing them to support an under-developed internal sense of personal adequacy. This deficit begins to drive an 'acquisition compulsion' to bolster self-esteem. [5]

The article closes with a number of specific suggestions for overcoming materialistic dependency, which include: focus on the personal qualities of others; find friends who appreciate you as a person; create a plan to reduce your debt; learn to enjoy life's simple pleasures; keep and appreciate what you have; and, finally, develop your spiritual life. Professor Stephen Marini, whom I quoted at the beginning of this chapter, describes the spiritual problem posed by materialism in these terms:

What's wrong with it? It extinguishes the spiritual life. Once you have narrowed down all the sources of meaning and value to "me, my family, my tribe, my elite," and "how much can I get for them?" then you are living in a morally diminished universe. Here is a case where more is literally less. One can argue that these values aren't bad in themselves. The problem is that there isn't anything else. Why does there need to be anything more? Everyone will have a different answer to that question. People will have an intuition that something is missing, but they won't have the foggiest idea of what that something is.

THE SUCCESS SYNDROME

He who dies with the most toys wins!

BUMPER STICKER

Our national obsession with success is what keeps us from admitting to failure (and profiting from the experience). Everyone wants to be successful, which is just as it should be. But few people are ever encouraged to think with any depth about what success might mean to them personally. The idea of success has become dissociated from the real flesh-and-blood individuals whose particular gifts and talents, relationships, histories, associations, and social and cultural contexts determine individually and uniquely what the word "success" may mean.

In the place of any personally meaningful understanding of success itself (ask your children if their school curriculum includes any substantial work on developing a personal understanding of success . . .), we are offered a variety of images of successful lifestyles. Television commercials present an incessant depiction of well-to-do, mostly young, mostly white, careerists, moving up to a Madison Avenue vision of the fullness of being. This includes sports cars and fine clothes, travel to soft white beaches or foreign lands. And all this is carried out with our credit cards, which provide us with access and clout and security the world over. Success means "the good life," and the more success the more life. Failure, on the other hand, implies a narrowing of experience and a gradual elimination of options — a kind of death-in-life. There is a flaw, however, in this simplistic equation of success to life and failure to death, for often it runs contrary to our experience. If we shun failure and allow ourselves to remain unaffected by its influence, we may find that moving from success to success is not to live a more expansive life but one that feels, somehow, strangely atrophied and misshapen. Success is feedback that we assume is positive but which, in fact, is only conservative: it confirms our hunches, what we already believe or suspect. It can also solidify our prejudices by locking us into an understanding of ourselves and the world that is outmoded or limited or too rigidly held or simply wrong. Success merely tells us that in *this* case, something worked the way we thought it would or hoped it would: success does not in itself have anything to do with confirming the inherent value or healthiness of our activity or attitude.

Many people travel through their lives ensconced in the protective comforts and habits of our culture, only inspired to begin questioning when an uninvited and unwanted crisis hits. Perhaps you know someone who has all the status symbols — the right job, the right house, the right car — yet never achieves a real sense of fulfillment. Perhaps you see this person in the mirror each morning. There are a few, however, who come to surprising clarity about themselves and their values early in life, learning to distinguish wheat from chaff in their own experiences of success and failure as shown in the following letter from a young woman cited below and in the story that follows it.

VICKY'S STORY

"I have been lucky enough to have had very few failures in my life so far (I'm 26), but I hope this account of my greatest failure will help you with your book.

"I quit a very well-paying job ($75,000) as manager of a retail art gallery because I realized that I was, deep down, not good at sales, managing employees, or playing the corporate power game. Six months later, here I am earning $10.00/hour as a temporary secretary, looking for a job as a college-level instructor of art history or museum curator in a very competitive job market. But I'm much happier.

"My one year of gallery management, rapid promotion, and good money earned the admiration of family and friends, but my outward appearance of success masked my true feelings: that I thought sales was vulgar, that I hated the high-pressure, deceitful sales tactics I was forced to use to make my quotas. My boss, a street-smart, tough woman, constantly reminded me of my inadequacies as a manager. One day, I couldn't take the pressure any more, no matter what the money was, and walked out.

"Looking back, I'm glad my failure only took one year. Many people are stuck in 20- to 30-year-long ures, which, like mine, have the outward appearance of success, until they retire and finally do what they really want.

"My failure clearly spelled out to me what I don't want in my career or my life (lots of money in exchange for high pressure and dishonesty), so that I can, one by one, rule in or out the variety of choices life gives me."

Pretty early in her adult life, through a single event, Vicky was able to clarify for herself the interests and values she felt drawn to pursue in her life. For many of us, this clarification takes place over many years and after many false starts. Thus far Vicky has had it relatively easy; she might even need to go through something like this again. It's worth noting that she quit not knowing what would happen next — such moves can be either foolhardy or courageous or a little of both. It takes disciplined self-examination to see clearly what is really going on. The process of working through the confusing clouds of family history, social background, cultural influences and personal experience is just that — a process — which hopefully leads to greater self-understanding and a more fulfilling life. In the story which follows, Jonathan outlines such a journey of self-discovery.

JONATHAN'S STORY

Long and lean, Jonathan seems so relaxed he almost melts into the chair. At 37, his life has included many false starts and changed directions, which he now regards as useful events that led him to his current home, in a lovely oceanfront city, and to the work he loves.

"As a kid I worked like hell to make the grade and do the right thing and please people. When I didn't, I heard about it. When I did, I didn't hear about it. So the idea of failure loomed prominently in my psyche from a very early age.

"I decided about halfway through the summer of my junior year in high school that I'd better find out what I'm supposed to do with my life. I knew it was going to have to be something very important, if it was to satisfy my family's and my own expectations for me. If I was going to do something important, I thought, I'd better get my shit together. So I decided to be a doctor — I knew that would be socially, morally, and economically compatible with the values and lifestyle I had grown up with. Once I got to college I started pre-med classes, and I did terribly. Although I had been an honor roll student in high school, and continued to do well in my other courses in college, I struggled horribly with the pre-med courses, and failed exams for the first time in my life. But I had a goal in mind, so I made myself push through it. In my junior year of college I started visiting medical schools, and by just looking around I realized what I had gotten myself into. I saw that the environment I was stepping into was unemotional and unsupportive, it felt alien and unfriendly, and I decided that I was not going to learn much about healing myself or about health by going to medical school. I had already done the pre-med tests, I had applications in to several schools, and I had to say screw it — this isn't for me. I didn't even have enough energy after that to finish my last quarter of organic chemistry. I just abandoned the whole idea of being a doctor, and felt a tremendous sense of failure.

"I started casting about for another direction, still feeling that I had to be a success on the terms I had grown up with — to fit into the culture in a way that meant achievement, superiority, affluence. So I went instead to a graduate program in international relations. It was almost ridiculously easy to get into this very competitive program; I felt as though the universe had opened the door for me. But this program was a tremendous struggle as well. The only classes I did well in were the classes involving international relations and human problems. The theory, economics and such I did much less well in. But I still wasn't willing to notice the signs; I just suffered through the schooling and then managed to land a plum job working for a major international bank — on Wall Street, no less. My heart was telling me, 'You don't want to do this!' but my mind was saying, 'Look what a great job you've landed! You've got to take it!' Of course, the intellect won out.

"Finally, I was in line with my family and friends — good job, real 'yuppie' lifestyle. But after finishing the training program at the bank, forces were at work both externally and internally that led me to resign. Externally, I couldn't communicate with my supervisor, who was extremely autocratic and ultimately wanted me fired, and although I was offered a position elsewhere within the firm I didn't feel I could function in that environment. On an internal level, I needed to be doing something closer to my heart. I wanted to do work I could believe in, and I wanted relationships with people — both working and personal — that were more nurturing and satisfying. But even though it was my choice to leave, it meant failure. As I later learned, no one in their right mind ever resigns from a job unless you have a better one lined up, and I didn't consider that, nor did I care. When I resigned they were shocked, they asked me to take some time and reconsider. But I think it was an inevitable decision, and lucky for me that it happened so quickly — better after six months than six years, because I still had enough resilience and wasn't yet locked into a mortgage, or lifestyle, or other responsibilities that would have rendered me less flexible.

"This experience sent me spiraling inside, and I had to sort through possible choices of what to do.

Here I was, living in New York, carrying around a tremendous sense of failure. All of a sudden I had nothing in common with any of my friends and colleagues. Failure can actually lead you to completely change your life, and even the form of your life can be completely changed — you don't see the same people, don't care about the same things, don't want the same things. That's very scary. What's so devastating is that in order to grow it may mean letting go of some of the patterns with which you've identified yourself completely. I had to let go of trying to fit into the signed, sealed, approved world. I also ended up letting go of some friendships that were completely tied to that world. I felt a lot of loss, and the void wasn't filled immediately.

"Finding work that suited me didn't happen quickly. I continued to make decisions I had to unmake later. I eventually ended up in a part of the country I feel much more comfortable in. When the time was right, I resurrected my old interest in medical school, but this time my choice was much more in line with my own sense of self. I trained in an intensive, four-year program in naturopathic medicine — it is a discipline that combines working with the body, mind and spirit, using conventional diagnostic techniques and clinical skills but with the addition of incorporating natural therapeutics, such as herbal, nutritional, and psychological care. I now have a private practice, and I find it's very meaningful work, and very helpful to others as well as to myself. I sense a vocation for myself here that is philosophically and spiritually in harmony with me and with the planet.

"I still have some pretty deep patterns of failure, and I experience them on an ongoing basis. For example, I'm dealing with one right now. I just finished a program of training in Chinese medicine. Acupuncture has been an integral part of my plan for about six years, and in many ways my practice won't be in full bloom until I become licensed to provide this service. In a recent licensure exam taken by 21 healthcare professionals, 18 were really well qualified, including 6 physicians from China, several of whom had been practicing for over 20 years. It was a pass/fail exam, and 17 of us failed. Clearly, there is something wrong with a system in which such highly qualified people were denied licensure. Well, I've been struggling with this, and trying to reframe it in a way that allows me to go past the point of labeling it 'failure.' I've been meeting with others who failed this test, and we've been coalescing our forces to try to resolve the fact that the exam given to us was arbitrary, unjust and incompetent. And we are doing something about it — we've put together a group letter, which 16 people signed. We're also trying to look at the underlying dynamic that has produced the result we've experienced. We're researching the department that sponsors the test to see how they work. . . . If we failed in any sense on this test, we failed in our ability to negotiate the system. Now, we're working to rectify that in a non-confrontational manner, trying to abide by the process the state has in place for resolving these issues. [As we went to press, we learned that this group presented the results of their research to the state board, who decided to eliminate the state exam in favor of the national exam. Jonathan is now licensed to practice acupuncture.]

"I think in our society, failure is a part of our cultural language — our culture believes in the duality of life, that you're either a success or a failure. And to the degree that a person defines him or herself by those criteria, it is very real and very powerful, it's all encompassing. You either have success — completely fortifying — or failure — completely devastating. But when a person gets a certain amount of experience and wisdom in life, other parts of the self rather than the conditioned, rational life speak loud enough so that they begin to question success and, conversely, to question failure. And at that point, I think the poles begin to approach each other, they're not as divergent as they seemed.

"But if we, in this culture, choose to describe life in terms of this paradigm of polarities, it's important to love both. Our whole culture is success oriented — dress for success, look successful, act successful, be successful. But the more we focus on just winning, the more power we're giving to the opposite response, so that when we don't win, we crash.

"When I was younger I identified very easily with the societal idea of failure. I would set myself up, crash, and then consider myself finished. Now I feel that failure is a pretty ongoing process — an integral part of living. My failures now are smaller and more frequent, because they're a more integrated part of my experience. I don't deny the feeling so much that it builds up into a huge collapse. Our culture prefers the devastating blow to the incremental change, so for me this more flexible approach to failure has been slow in coming. To a certain degree I've learned to look at thoughts of failure as just thoughts, like other thoughts ... they come and go. I can do that best when I accept ideas and practices outside of our culture. I find that meditation really is helpful to accept thoughts just as thoughts, not to give them so much emphasis that we're crippled by them.

"Failure used to mean 'You're not good enough.' Now, it's simply an indication that it's time to move in some way. It's like a flag, or beacon, saying, 'Time to change ... time to shift.' And I'm getting better at reading the signs."

To a large extent the society in which we live plays a role in our struggle with failure. This is true despite the evident wisdom in Marcus Aurelius' observation that, "If you are distressed by anything external, the pain is not due to the thing itself, but to your estimate of it; and this you have the power to revoke at any moment." In ways that may not always be obvious to us, society nonetheless shapes our attempts to understand the questions and formulate our answers when we think about success and failure. We are bound to this society, and this is not a tie that can easily be dissolved. Even a radical critique of society, one that spurns conventional definitions of success and failure, is bound to it in opposition. We can leave it, but we cannot leave it as if it weren't there.

So, within the context of the culture in which we live, we struggle individually with the problem of failure. Denis Waiteley has written, "One of the best ways to properly evaluate and adapt to the many environmental stresses of life is to simply view them as normal. The adversity and failures in our lives, if adapted to and viewed as normal corrective feedback to use to get back on target, serve to develop in us an immunity against anxiety, depression, and the adverse responses to stress." It is the experience of this struggle — occurring uniquely to each one who engages in it, involving challenges and the potential rewards surprisingly waiting at the heart of failure — that we will now explore.

INTRODUCTION TO THE EXERCISES IN THIS BOOK

To do the exercises profitably, it is important to set aside some quiet time in a place by yourself so that you can give this process your full attention. You will need a small notebook as well. If you have someone close to you with whom you can safely share and explore these exercises, please do so! We can hear much about ourselves through the eyes and hearts of others, if we are discerning.

The process we will follow in these exercises has three parts: "Recollection, Recreation, Empowerment." First you will look back over your life experiences. Then you will create a new vision of your own life. Finally you will give strength to that vision through newly acquired self-understanding and personal affirmation. That's the theory! In reality it's never perfectly neat and orderly as a process, but don't worry. The exercises are meant to provoke both fresh thoughts and feelings — always a somewhat unsettling experience. There are no right answers; only you can judge when you have reflected or written enough. Keep your sense of humor handy. Don't be afraid to digress. But look upon the exercises as a multi-step process that you *will* finish. Keep a sense of hopeful anticipation. You will be surprised at what you discover!

FIRST EXERCISE

A. As a young person what were your "inherited ideas" about success? How was success understood in your family, in your school, in your life outside of school?

B. What were your "inherited ideas" about failure? Was failure talked about in the settings listed above? If so, how? If not, why not? Did you know any people who had experienced failure? How were they treated?

C. Look back on what you have written in response to questions A and B. How has your understanding of success and failure changed over the years through your own life experience? What are the important qualities you look for in success today? What meaning does failure have for you now?

FAILURE and the INDIVIDUAL
The Stages of Failure

Turning and turning in the widening gyre
The falcon cannot hear the falconer;
Things fall apart; the centre cannot hold;
Mere anarchy is loosed upon the world,
The blood-dimmed tide is loosed, and everywhere
The ceremony of innocence is drowned;
The best lack all conviction, while the worst
Are full of passionate intensity.

WILLIAM BUTLER YEATS
[from "The Second Coming"]

THE WORDS OF THE POET YEATS describe, with dramatic concision, the spiraling confusion one feels as one tumbles into the experience of failure. Like the falcon flying in an ever-widening circle around the falconer, who calls to it from the center of its orbit, the one who is experiencing the "mere anarchy" of failure may feel very far removed from the personal center, the authentic self, the basis for confident and competent action in the world. The structures of the familiar can no longer be thrown up against the onrush of events. And, as in all cases where one's personal center is threatened, fear — as though one's very life were in jeopardy — accompanies the confusion.

"I felt as though the ground was opening beneath me! Like the world was going to swallow me up!" "I was in free fall!" "It was weird. I sort of felt as though the world was somehow less real, like I was disconnected, except of course when it came crashing in on me. It was that kind of alternating experience: sometimes I was 'out of it,' sometimes I couldn't get away from it."

These comments typify the feelings of many we have spoken to about the experience of failure. Suddenly, a violent disruption in the normal patterns of life threatens an individual with an overwhelming sense of powerlessness. In the face of defeat one feels that all options and opportunities to act constructively have disappeared.

THE PRECIPITATING EVENT

Often a particular event precipitates the onset of the failure experience. A pink slip, or a rising tide of red ink on a company balance sheet are typical. So is an ultimatum from a loved one, or a divorce. Sometimes there may be a persistent physical manifestation — a rash, a headache — a breaking into consciousness of a problem that demands attention. Once the breach is opened, there is no going back.

"Everything started unraveling all at once. Before, I was always able to pull a rabbit out of my hat, you know, perform some kind of miracle to keep things together. This time it all hit me together! Things just started moving faster and faster. I couldn't control it."

Circumstances which may have been deteriorating for some time can no longer be contained. In one case we know about, a woman who was experiencing the collapse of her business — brought about in part by employee theft but largely because of her own alienation from the work — told us that from her present vantage point she is amazed at how long she held on "without getting the message." She describes herself as receiving all sorts of clues, from increasingly rigid behavior in the office and a growing desire to avoid coming to work, to a recurrent outbreak of an almost symbolic physical ailment.

KAREN'S STORY

"On my company's first anniversary, I decided to go out and reward myself. It had been a very successful start-up. We had a major high-profile client who had kept us busy. On the strength of that account we had begun to fashion a comfortable foundation on which to build the company's future. We had a small office and several employees and things looked bright indeed. So I wrote myself a check, and with that money bought a nice watch, something I very much needed. For me that watch was a symbol of having 'arrived' as a business woman.

"The truth, however, was that things were about to unravel. The bigger the company grew, the more tenuous it was, financially. I had taken on more employees, whose production in terms of sales was poor. We became involved in several unprofitable projects and — as we discovered later — one of our staff members was embezzling funds. Eventually we were affected by the area's economic downturn — good clients began postponing or downsizing projects as belt-tightening measures. But even though our billings couldn't support the staff size, I kept hoping that our situation would improve and we continued to operate with an unreasonable overhead. As the months went by the losses piled up and I felt trapped.

"It began to feel like a hopeless situation. The work continued to be of a high standard, but the business wasn't working and I had lost heart. The atmosphere around the office grew more and more negative and pessimistic. After I finally began to lay people off, my heart went out of it completely. All I really wanted to do was get away.

"Of course, my mood affected everyone around me. I was depressed at home and reluctant to keep up with friends for fear that they would be critical of me. I had always been successful in everything I had tried. I could not understand what was going on in my life. Worse, I could not see any way out. My husband and I worked out endless schemes and strategies for saving the company or even closing it without a major disaster. But it didn't seem possible. Every scenario was worse than the last. I felt I had to hang on, even though hanging on was only making things worse. I was completely stuck and I hated it!

"Then something curious happened. One day my wrist broke out in an angry red rash. It got to the point where I couldn't wear my watch any longer because it was too painful. This was the same watch I had bought with pride just three years earlier. When I took the watch off, however, the rash went away. Then, every time I put that watch on, the rash would return. It was as if wearing that watch symbolized everything that I now wanted to be rid of: the responsibility for running the business, my responsibility to employees, my concern for what other people in the business community thought of me, even the desire to be 'a success.' My body was telling me what my ego would not admit. The more I ignored this sign, the more others crowded in, demanding my attention. I couldn't sleep, I was exhausted, I felt constantly on the brink of tears, and I started having outbreaks of hives all over my body whenever I was under stress — which at that point was most of the time.

"This was just the tip of the iceberg. As I became increasingly emotionally distraught and incapacitated, I realized I needed some help, so for the first time in my life I put myself in counseling. This was the beginning of a tremendous period of learning about myself. Gradually, I grew to realize that 'the real me' had over the years almost completely disappeared behind the roles that I felt I was required to play.

"As I grew reacquainted with myself, I began to close the company down."

DENIAL AND RESISTANCE

Often those who are fighting off the looming crisis "receive a sign." The woman in the story above is fortunate indeed that a harmless rash on her wrist was enough to catch her attention and trigger the beginning of an important period of self-examination and reflection. Was she slow to recognize her impending failure? Hindsight is not a very sympathetic judge, nor is the judge who observes such a situation from a safely removed vantage point. Hindsight says yes, she was slow; you as the reader of her story may have seen early on that she was going to crash. But what of it? The individual experiencing failure is *inside* the experience and for a long time, as it builds to crescendo, cannot see it for what it is. Karen's story, compared to the others collected for this book, is normal. If anything, the dramatic sign she received (or produced for herself), the rash, indicates that she was actually beginning to cope with her failure — by becoming aware of it, by *acknowledging* it.

More common is the slow deterioration in the quality of life of those who refuse to acknowledge what is happening to them. Although it may be insensitive to compare people's misfortunes, it does seem that those whose normal lives have been brought to a sudden and inescapable standstill are in some ways better off than those whose failure crisis has become an attenuated dull fact of life. Better the rash you can't hide from than the headache you can pretend isn't there. Stuck in a condition of homeostasis, an individual may not be aware that anything is particularly wrong, but neither is he or she aware of anything especially right. In fact, the ability to be aware at all gradually becomes compromised through an endless repetition of minor crises and dull responses. Perpetuating this lethal cycle that brings deadliness into the midst of life is the whole arsenal of denial — much of which is tacitly condoned by society. Through the abuse of alcohol or drugs, the addiction to work, or the distractions offered by endless amusements or superficial relationships, one can indefinitely resist the awareness that this is not a life worthy of the name — an awareness which itself, if recognized, would be powerful enough to raise the possibility of change. However this denial is achieved — through a willed daze of apathy or a pervasive undirected anger — its ultimate effect is hostile to growth and well-being.

There are times, of course, when one is simply unable to face up to experience: the sense of crisis may be so severe and so fresh and the pain so great that a "strategic retreat" is required. However, it must not be forgotten that this can only be a temporary retreat. The challenge to continue the journey, to continue the struggle, to make sense out of what happens to us, calls us on.

OCCASION NOT CAUSE

It is simplistic to assert that people get what's coming to them. Although, there do seem to be instances where a certain poetic appropriateness exists between a particular form of disease and an individual's personality, habits, and lifestyle, it has become fashionable to make these connections in absolute terms, as if they represented a cause and effect relationship. When such "diagnoses" are made on another's behalf, they are clearly misguided. First of all, this smacks of spiritual reductionism — a translation of all phenomena into metaphysical terms. Second, rather than conveying the gift of understanding, these attempts may come across as an assignment of blame to someone who would do better with a little genuine compassion.

The problem is that this reductionism is retrospective. It attempts to look back over a life and explain current experience in terms of the past. Sometimes this can be done, and sometimes it cannot. What it tends to ignore, however, is the extreme complexity of even the most ordinary experience. There is always the possibility that one's experience may be decisively determined by factors that are entirely arbitrary. If I am sick tomorrow, it may be simply because a lone germ was carried to me quite by chance from someone else's sneeze.

Having said this, it is equally clear that even without an obvious causal link, crises of all kinds can provide *occasions* for self-discovery and growth. Here the view is not merely retrospective but prospective as well. One looks backwards not to explain the present, but to understand the unfolding future. A frequent account from those who have survived a heart attack or a stroke is that during the period of their convalescence they began a complete top-to-bottom reevaluation of their lives. In Wendy Williams' book, *The Power Within*, stories of exceptional patients who struggle with life-threatening diseases like cancer offer example after example of how the experience of failure — in this case the failure of the physical organism — leads to new life *because of* and not in spite of their experience.

Before cancer, I had been having trouble communicating with my kids, probably because I was too busy with my own business to really listen to them. During those first weeks and months, when death felt so imminent, I spent many sleepless nights because of medications. I began to use those nights to write letters to my daughters at college, trying to let them know some of the things I was feeling but couldn't talk about.

One day my oldest daughter telephoned. We talked pleasantly and then I passed the phone to my wife. Later, Linda told me what my daughter had said.

"I know Dad's sick," she said hesitantly, "but I like the new Dad better."

For the first time in my life, I began to look critically at that blind drive to achieve that had motivated me for almost 40 of my nearly 50 years.[1]

The following story brings together several of the strands of our discussion. Here the cause of the failure experience was discovered to be physiological, though for some time a psychological cause was hypothesized and sought. What is more important, however, is that the experience of failure was the occasion for important changes in Tom's life.

TOM'S STORY

Tom, an easygoing, sandy-haired, bearded man, travels from his home in the mountains to two part-time jobs — one as a counselor in a pastoral counseling center in a nearby town, the other as a program director for a lakeside retreat center. Sometimes, over the phone, his gravelly voice gives the impression of someone in his 60s or 70s — actually, he is in his 40s, struggling with a debilitating medical condition called spasmodic dysphonia. He tells a story in which the failure of his voice led to the loss of his job as a pastor and to the discovery of hidden parts of himself.

"Perhaps I should start by explaining that I had never intended to be an ordained minister. My first love was working with young people, and I had planned to become a high school youth counselor. I decided to train in a seminary because I felt strongly that there needed to be a spiritual element included in my work with young people, and in the process of doing the field work and working in churches as part of my training, I ran across some great role models and became enthusiastic about working in the church setting. My career direction gradually shifted, and I decided to become an ordained minister. I took a job as associate pastor with a special focus on youth ministry and I enjoyed it. After a few years, however, my wife and I decided we wanted some experience working overseas. There was a congregation in Sydney, Australia, that was looking for a pastor — someone who would look after that church and two others associated with it.

"I'd never been a particularly fluent speaker and I was untrained in the proper use of the voice. In fact, I'd had some strange problems. As a child, I could never blow out birthday candles or do the crawl swimming, because I had trouble getting the breathing right. At the same time, I had a tendency to project my voice from the throat, rather than from what's called 'the facial mask' — the resonant chamber that is made up of the bones and open spaces of the face. But I never expected that my voice would play a deciding role in my career direction.

"After several months in Australia, preaching up to three times a week, my voice started to get hoarse and tired. That seemed reasonable, because it was a rigorous speaking schedule, but as it continued to get worse, with a breaking and strangled quality, I began to look for solutions. The harder I looked, the more my voice seemed to disintegrate. I started by working with actors, then speech therapists; finally I started seeing what ended up being a string of physicians and counselors. No one could solve the puzzle. After several years in Australia, we returned to the States, where I took what I thought would be a less taxing position as associate pastor, but my voice continued to plague me. A reduced speaking schedule didn't help; new breathing and speaking techniques didn't help; voice rest didn't help. Eventually, after about eight years, I resigned and decided to return to my original career idea, which was school counseling. That turned out to be even more difficult — with the classroom expectations and the counseling combined, it was more stressful than the church in terms of my voice. I managed to hang on for two years before needing another change.

"My spirits were very low. I had enjoyed that job — I liked the kids, I liked working with the parents and teachers, and I loved the schedule because it put me in synch with that of my wife, who is a school librarian, and with my daughter. It felt like a big sacrifice to give up all that and to have nothing to look forward to, but it turned out that new opportunities were about to unfold. I discovered that my loss of voice, which I had come to believe was a psychological problem, was actually due to a neurological weakness. The disorder, called spasmodic dysphonia, is characterized by involuntary, uncontrollable muscle spasms. There are other kinds of dysphonias, which cause facial tics, writer's cramp, and other spastic physical movements, but spasmodic dysphonia causes the vocal chords to go into spasm, leading to strangled, gravelly, or breaking speech. While stress can bring on the symptoms, it doesn't cause the disorder. My neurological weakness may have been inherited or caused by a bout of encephalitis when I was seven.

"After 15 years of struggle, a treatment has been discovered: an injection of a minute quantity of botulin toxin into the vocal chords. It doesn't cure the problem but does relieve the symptoms for about four to six months at a time. I'm now on a regimen where I have an injection about two or three times a year and it makes a tremendous difference. I'm not cured, but I am helped for the present until something better is discovered. And it has been a tremendous relief to know that my condition is medical, not psychological, and that I hadn't brought it on myself and my family.

"As it has turned out, I have been able to put together interesting work very soon after leaving the school. My speech therapist offered me an office in her building, and I set up a private counseling practice, which was started with a few youths and adults

I had been working with in my former job. It's been very rewarding. I function as a 'wounded healer' — based on my own experience of being wounded and in the process of healing, there's much more empathy within me for people's sufferings. Being in touch with my own sense of loss — not just of my voice but in other areas as well — I am able to be more present for clients who themselves are suffering losses.

"At the same time as I decided to do some part-time counseling, I learned there was an opening at an ecumenical retreat center nearby for someone to develop workshops and other programming. I have been there on a part-time basis ever since. That has opened up a whole new world — an international array of fascinating people and interesting programs. I've been there for four years, and I wouldn't trade that time. I wouldn't have traded my past jobs either, difficult as they were. These experiences give me considerable hope for the future, whatever it holds. With the economy the way it is, my wife or I could lose a job at any time, but we have lots of interests and places we'd like to go. We've taken risks and landed on our feet before and I feel confident and comfortable that something will work out. I have learned to build strong support systems of family, friends and fellow journeyers wherever I go. A relationship to God and church play an important part.

"The loss of my voice has also led to some changes in my inner life. Fifteen years of struggle and increasing isolation have left me more serious and thoughtful. I am much more aware of personal stress and take steps to avoid it. I always had a tendency to be outer-directed — now I'm more interested in exploring my interior life as well. The whole focus for

> my work over the last few years — either in counsel-
> ing or through the workshops I develop — is to give
> people an opportunity to do what I'm doing — to
> find inner direction, 'God within.' I enjoy making time
> for solitude, for silent time. I am less social — I tend
> to save more of my time for family and friends. I
> have taken the opportnity to be a more conscious par-
> ent and spouse, to spend more time and attention on
> these relationships. Ultimately, my relationships have
> deepened and strengthened. Reaching inward gives
> me more energy to reach out to others and the world.
> I feel I'm in a good place now."

As Tom's story shows, a severe physical disability can
bring on an apparent spiral of defeats and losses. The disability in Tom's case had no effect on his desire or willingness to work hard but neither did his hard work or his
sincerity avoid the failures and losses. As in most of the
stories you'll read in this book, the plot line in this one is
years long. It took Tom — and his family — years to recognize not just his medical problem for what it actually is
but years also to recognize the linkage between his handi-
cap and the outcome of his experience. The tendency was
to assume he had a psychosomatic problem, that his failures
were "all in his head." Such a reading of Tom's dilemma is
reductionist in the worst way; he was fortunate not to have
gotten hooked on this line of interpretation. And fortunate
to have discovered — through new, objective information
— that he had a treatable medical problem, not an untreat-
able, characterological proclivity for professional failure. It
should not pass without noting either that Tom's transformation into a thriving, happier man involved paying greater
attention to his interior life — call it psychological or spiritual, as you please. Many of the stories presented here take

such a turn, and though the storytellers' vocabulary may vary, the message is much the same. Tom's failures, physical and professional, provided the opportunity for his re-evaluation and growth.

Now we turn to the ways in which we — as physical, psychological and spiritual beings — respond to the experience of failure.

PHYSICAL REACTIONS

"During this whole period [of crisis] I pigged out. I ate everything I could get my hands on: bread and butter, popcorn, subs, pizza, candy bars, 'triple thick shakes.' This really wasn't like me. I had gone on the occasional junk food binge in the past, but in general I like food that's pretty healthy. This was different: this was serious junk food!"

When crisis does hit, it affects all the important areas of life: the physical, the psychological and emotional, and the spiritual. On the physical level, for instance, it is common for individuals to begin to overeat and to be careless about diet and nutrition. For instance, foods high in saturated fats, which produce a lethargic and listless effect on an individual's awareness, may be consumed to achieve a mild narcosis, a presumed escape route. Alternately, a general depression and listlessness may lead to undernourishment. One may be too preoccupied to eat or eating may produce nausea.

Alcohol abuse is also very common. The elaborate social rituals, powerful merchandising, and the intricate practices surrounding the consumption of liquor lend both an aura of respectability on the one hand and an aura of dangerous, macho risk-taking on the other. As such, alcohol is extremely susceptible to abuse. One couple reported that — to avoid facing the reality of a business failure — their alcohol consumption climbed to a routine half-a-magnum of white wine every night, which they drank in front of the television — a deadening combination under the best of circumstances.

Physical exercise may fall off. Those whose routines normally include vigorous activities — jogging, trips to the gym, tennis, and so forth — may begin to stay home or find other less active pastimes, such as movies or television. The reasons for this may involve several different factors at once. It may be that by staying at home one is seeking to avoid others who may ask awkward questions about the failure no one really wants to discuss, or, worse, may slide into awkward silences. Or the surprising physical inertia may simply be one element of a "system-wide" shut down. One woman told us: "I slept a lot. By two in the afternoon I would be wondering if I could get away with just going to bed." And another recalled: "I drank more, I slept more, I exercised not-at-all."

Alternately, physical exercise may dramatically increase. "I became an exercise junkie. I threw myself into it, to get my mind off everything else." Instead of lying around at home, one becomes a resident of the health club or spends hours jogging or swimming. The reason for this extreme activity lies in a perceived need to keep busy, to remain distracted. (And of course the resultant surge of endorphins that are released into the bloodstream after intense physical exertion provides an actual high that may momentarily chase away the blues.)

What determines whether this behavior is dysfunctional is the question of motivation and balance. There's no point in arguing that plenty of exercise is a bad thing! If the exercise increases one's ability to deal with difficult circumstances, then it can only help. Exercise is usually relaxing, and a relaxed person can think more clearly. If it occupies so much of a person's time and energy that no opportunity remains for tackling the problem at hand, then it is a signal that life is out of balance. "Running" — in any form — away from failure actually gets you nowhere.

PSYCHOLOGICAL REACTIONS

We have suggested in this book that failure and deception are intimately linked. How these two are connected is determined differently in each individual's life. My own failure was the result of my unwillingness and, eventually, inability to see what was inauthentic in my understanding of myself and my direction in life. The inauthenticity lay in my mistaken habit of thinking I was obligated to pursue a life based on values I really did not believe in. To take another example, one may experience failure in a marriage if the relationship ceases to offer the partners a context which supports the full expression of their identities. If you can't be who you really are with the one you're supposed to love, you'd better start taking a serious, compassionate look at it. In other words, failure ensues if the relationship is either founded on or has fallen into inauthenticity.

Once any failure is exposed, there is an upheaval during which the individual is called upon to decide what to do with the new bad news. It will appear that there are choices: that both engagement with the problem and evasion at all costs are equal possibilities. The latter, however, is a false hope. In fact, there is only one choice worth making — the decision to sit up and really pay attention to one's experience — a decision one may make now or later. But the longer one waits, the more painful it becomes even to acknowledge failure or to make difficult and meaning-ful changes to get out of it. The longer one lives with inauthenticity, the greater its seeming reality appears. Counterfeit though an inauthentic life may be, it is never-theless, "life as we know it." It can never be easy to shake off the illusion, and the more one identifies with a partial or misconceived understanding of the self or of the world, the more one feels that to give up the counterfeit is to sac-rifice the self. In more abrupt terms, it feels like death.

Therefore, at one time or another, transforming failure into the fruits of failure requires upheaval.

On the psychological level, people in the crisis of failure may react in a number of ways. In fact, over the course of a failure experience, most people have a multifaceted reac-tion. The experience of failure affects emotional balance, behavior, thought patterns, relationships, even perception. The one common feature is the consuming, all-encompass-ing intensity of a failure crisis. It overwhelms life-as-usual.

Emotional Stress

"I couldn't leave the house for six weeks." — SAM

"I discovered depression." — BERT

"I became suicidal." — ANNE

In the depths of the experience of failure, emotions can run the gamut, from deep lethargy, depression and suicidal feelings, to restlessness and agitated excitability. People commonly experience strong feelings of rage, terror, shame, humiliation or hopelessness. Some describe months of feel-ing that any effort is futile. Time seems either to drag on interminably, or to race ahead, seemingly out of control.

These phases may also move in a progression. An individual may run maniacally ahead of the realization of failure and then crash into depression when his physical resources have been exhausted. In any case, the customary emotional patterns of life — which, to be sure, are never perfectly stable or consistent — are thrown off balance.

In the midst of a failure crisis, any attempt to conduct business as usual may be negated by the onslaught of fear, which paralyzes us into inactivity. This anxiety often is experienced as the fear of being discovered or found out. In a society that extolls its successes and denies its failures, it is understandable that someone who considers himself a failure would be very anxious that someone else might find out and reveal his inadequacies to the world. Feelings of failure can be so vivid and immediate that it is impossible to believe that they might not be conspicuous to everyone on the outside. One woman recalled, "When my husband left, I was so vulnerable. I was certain that people could see how raw I felt. I felt sure they knew."

Coping Behavior

"I felt totally alone. After my marriage failed, it took all my energy simply to survive, to get food on the table for myself and my kids. I coped. " — ALICE

A person under stress frequently resorts to coping. Often this is a necessary first reaction. It needs to be recognized as such, and one should resist the exhortations of well-meaning friends to "cheer up" or "get over it." Artificially modifying one's behavior in response to such influences from the outside only compound the failure, for such modifications pile deception on top of deception.

The changes in emotional tone and range that accompany the crisis of failure affect and exacerbate our state of anxiety. Those around us may observe "self-defeating" attitudes or behavior. These are not necessarily intended to create or perpetuate further failure, yet, as part of the dynamic of our interactions, these behaviors represent us as failures to others.

Once we find ourselves locked into relationships where we suspect we are being negatively assessed, then coping may take the form — at least temporarily — of "strategic retreat." Alice (quoted just above) faced a three-year process in which the devastating effects of a failed marriage meant that all she could do was cope. Yet she did so very effectively, moving her family to a new town, finding a new job, and slowly figuring out how be a single parent. Once she was back on her feet, she was able to look beyond mere survival, and was ready to seek out new relationships and work that suited her more fully.

"Just managing to cope" may strike you as being a long way from having fixed or solved the problem which appears, at the outset, as the cause of your failure. But we should not be too quick to dismiss or devalue the process of "just coping." When the mind, the heart, the soul — call them what you will — have work to do, such as serious self-examination and reconsideration of many external influences on the self as well, this work is slow going and will not be pushed. It has its own timetable which may bear little or no relationship to whatever your conscious mind has set up as a deadline by which time you are determined to have fixed the problem, to feel fine again. "Just coping" is analogous to the pain one feels when, say, an ankle has been sprained: the pain is a natural splint. Its message is: whoa there, ease up, slow down and give the interior energies of blood and enzymes and hormones their chance to do some good healing work. If you deny the pain, ignore the splint, miss the message, chances are you'll sprain the ankle all over again.

Thinking Patterns

One doesn't discover new lands without consenting to lose sight of the shore for a very long time.

ANDRE GIDE

Confusion is a nearly universal aspect of the failure experience. One can have a deep and alarming sense that all the mooring lines have been cast overboard, that there is no point of reference around which thought can organize in meaningful patterns. Ideas seem jumbled, in turmoil, and repetitive, even obsessive. Time and time again the same thoughts return, but there is no progress in them. People who are in crisis can even feel that the need to interact with others in a rational, organized manner is a threat — they either can't do it, or don't want to.

Our ability to create or imagine new possibilities is lost. Our will to engage the present or plan the future is set aside. We are less able to solve problems that previously would have caused us little difficulty, and, naturally, the effect this produces is an increase in tension, just what the person in failure does not need.

Relationships

"I continued to develop my shut-up-ness and to bottle up my anger, which exploded only in the safety of home, at my wife and kids." — SEAN

Frequently, individuals in crisis will retreat, isolating themselves from family, friends, and coworkers. In some cases, this isolation is actual, a physical removal of oneself from ordinary interactions and activities. At others, the isolation will be an internal exile in which the external patterns of life appear as normal but the individual has withdrawn to some deep internal concealment. One way or another, alienation from the world of genuine relationship and creative activity increases to a state of isolation and inertia. The person in a failure crisis may be stuck here for some time.

Paradoxically, there is the potential that such isolation and inactivity can provide an opportunity for quiet reflection and useful solitude. There is no formula for this conversion, but later chapters will suggest some helpful approaches.

Perception

"I was a bundle of nerves. Everything seemed to be running in fast-forward." — JUDY

Failure leads to a conviction that we lack inner resources or have an inability to find or use the positive aspects of ourselves. Our perception grows muddy. We can't see what's inside us; we're not ready to see what's outside. Furthermore, the (alleged) fact of our failure, charged as it is with emotional potency, exercises a correspondingly powerful force on any new information that presents itself to our senses. New events and experiences are organized to fit into the negative self-concept: I am a failure, therefore, whatever occurs to me will likewise end in failure. One failure bleeds into another. This may occur even when to the outsider this negative "fit" is patently absurd. Eventually, this leads to a state where self-esteem, the foundation of our ability to act effectively in the world, is seriously compromised.

Self-Esteem

"I felt tremendously self-conscious and embarrassed."

— NADIA

"I tried to avoid talking about my failure. I was careful to steer the conversation away from anything that had to do with me." — MARTIN

Once an individual allows a sense of failure to shift *from* a judgment made, for whatever reason, on outside events and circumstances *to* a judgment about the worth or value or competence of the self, self-esteem is critically endangered.

Allowing one's self-esteem to become undermined by failure is a real and present danger in the failure experience. It is only the individual, finally, who can lift the sentence of failure from his existence. Friends, family, therapist, new employer, new lover: none can reverse the judgment an individual has made on himself. It's a *personal* decision and not everyone is able to unload that burden, at least not fully or quickly. A loss of self-esteem, which may bring the individual to believe that this sentence is somehow apt or deserved, can greatly prolong the crisis of failure.

There is then a quality of forgetting, of losing the memory of one's essential worth and value to others. A woman who had been a successful film producer in England found that there were, after moving to the United States, few opportunities for her to pursue her career in the city where she settled. At one point, having exhausted every possibility she could think of, she was forced to take a temporary job as a waitress in a deli. She told us that the worst part of her experience was that she began to forget that she had ever done anything else. Her work as an artist and a producer — an extremely important piece of her positive self-understanding — had faded into unreality. She told us how for months she could only think of herself as a waitress. Finally her crisis was so acute that it jolted her into a fresh recognition of her talent and abilities, which led her to discover new opportunities. But note the geometry of her story. She evidently had to go down, way down, before she could come back up.

SPIRITUAL REACTIONS

As with all crises, failure brings individuals up against the limits of their view of the world. Because a crisis is by its nature unstable and pushes toward a resolution, something has to change — either the view of the world or the viewer or both. The good news is that genuine spiritual growth tends in one direction: toward an increasing openness to life and a concomitant decrease in life-defeating strategies of evasion, self-deception and denial. The bad news is that this process is never painless. It is slow, piecemeal and subject to temporary reversals. You may need to step back and feel the pain again and reconfirm your decision to get out of it. We rarely get away with learning our lessons once; we practice using our new perceptions, again and again, feeling some of the failure-pain each time until we've really gotten the message into the marrow of our bones.

In his moving book *When Bad Things Happen To Good People*, Rabbi Harold Kushner describes how the illness and early death of his son threw him into a crisis of faith. The old notions he had been raised with — of a God who could be relied upon always to rescue his children in times of trial — vanished in the stark reality of his grief.

Like most people, my wife and I had grown up with an image of God as an all-wise, all-powerful parent figure who would treat us as our earthly parents did, or even better. If we were obedient and deserving, He would reward us. If we got out of line, He would discipline us, reluctantly but firmly. He would protect us from being hurt or from hurting ourselves, and would see to it that we got what we deserved in life.

Like most people, I was aware of the human tragedies that darkened the landscape — the young people who died in car crashes, the cheerful, loving people wasted by crippling diseases, the neighbors and relatives whose retarded or mentally ill children people spoke of in hushed tones. But that awareness never drove me to wonder about God's justice, or to question His fairness. I assumed that He knew more about the world than I did.

Then came that day in the hospital when the doctor told us about Aaron and explained what progeria meant. It contradicted everything I had been taught. I could only repeat over and over again in my mind, "This can't be happening. It is not how the world is supposed to work." Tragedies like this were supposed to happen to selfish, dishonest people whom I, as a rabbi, would then try to comfort by assuring them of God's forgiving love. How could it be happening to me, to my son, if what I believed about the world was true. [2]

After a long and difficult struggle, Rabbi Kushner was able to reconstruct an idea of God that allowed him to continue to believe. His new understanding did not attribute to God the qualities of providential omnipotence that are such a universal characteristic of God in popular piety. According to his reconstructed understanding, God cannot prevent life's misfortunes, but is always ready when those misfortunes strike to support us in our grief. This represented a more mature and more adequate understanding of what, for him, is ultimately important.

The spiritual dimension of the failure experience may reach into the very core of one's existence. A significant failure can call into question all of a person's sources of meaning and value. Whatever one's particular system of belief may be, the validity of these beliefs will be sorely tested. That which is adequate will stand up. That which is not will disintegrate. As Meister Ekhart observed: "Spiritual growth is a process of subtraction." It's as though as young people, hungry for learning and experience, we get filled up with a jumble of untested ideas, beliefs, prejudices, assumptions, tastes, and the like. The confidence and impetuousness of youth may rest precariously on this unsteady jumble. Spiritual growth, often achieved through the trial-by-fire of a crisis, like failure, turns out to be a stripping down to the minimum essential beliefs that last, that work in the sense that they shed the light of genuine understanding and acceptance. All the rest can be jettisoned. In any case, it is one's *current* understanding of what is meaningful that is at stake in a failure crisis. Even greater meaningfulness — hidden but at hand — is the potential reward.

THE VORTEX

To all new truths, or renovations of old truths, it must be as in the ark between the destroyed and the about-to-be renovated world. The raven must be sent out before the dove, and ominous controversy must precede peace and the olive wreath.

SAMUEL TAYLOR COLERIDGE
[quoted in *The Writings on the Wall*,
Terry Tillman, 1990]

Assembling from all these different areas of life — physical, psychological, and spiritual — a composite portrait of a man or a woman in these early stages of the failure crisis reveals a life that has to a very great extent come to resemble the opposites of contentment, peace of mind, and good health: physically lethargic and unresponsive, with senses either dulled or feverishly overstimulated, depressed, fearful, inward turning, cut off, shut off, shut down and alienated from the sources of meaning, value and purpose.

This picture may be extreme in the eyes of some. Not every one of us comes to this condition, or if we do, we do not stay there forever. On the other hand, there are fewer still who have not felt this way at one time or another.

As I describe in my own failure story in the Appendix, the weeks just prior to my confrontation with failure were characterized by intense, unremitting, and increasingly desperate thinking. I dreamed up scheme after scheme for holding off what I now see was inevitable. Many endure sleepless nights. Days spent pacing the floor. Or looking out store windows watching and waiting for customers who never came, turning over and over in their heads the questions, "What happens if I . . ." or "What do I do now?"

A vortex is a swirling mass — like a whirlpool or a tornado. On the outside there is boundless activity. But on the inside is a vacuum. And the greater the emptiness, at one's center, the more intense the circling thoughts all around it.

THE MYTH OF THE PHOENIX

Most people today will tell you, when you ask, that the phoenix is "that bird that rises from the ashes." Quite probably, this will be the only thing they can tell you about the fabulous bird. Yet the phoenix has a story as strange and wonderful as anything in mythology.

To begin with, the phoenix is unique. This means not only that no other bird is like him, but also that he cannot be rivalled even by another pheonix. For legend says that in all the world there is never more than one Bird of the Sun at a time. If you should be lucky enough to see one phoenix, you have seen them all — past, present, and future. The bird before you would have died a million deaths before this moment and would have a million times as many lifetimes yet to come, always being reborn, always remaining the same.

The period of the phoenix's strange life is definitely fixed, although various versions of the legend differ as to just what that period is. It is most commonly given as five hundred years. For all the days of his life the phoenix lives in a deathless and sorrowless land somewhere in the East, a land never visited by mortal man. The phoenix is a bird of peace. During his five hundred years in paradise he eats no living thing, but feeds on air.

At last, however, weary with the burden of the centuries, the phoenix leaves his home and flies westward. In the groves of Arabia he loads his wings with aromatic spices — frankincense, cinnamon and myrrh. Then, flying on, he comes to the coast of Phoenicia on the Mediterranean, the land that bears his name. In the top of the tallest palm tree he builds a nest of spices, and in the nest he waits through the long night.

Just at dawn, the phoenix turns to the east and begins to sing, a song not heard in the world for five hundred years. So sweet is the song that the stars, the earth, and the sun itself stop and listen. Then the first rays of the sunrise strike the nest and set it afire. Still singing, the phoenix is burnt to ashes in this funeral pyre of his own making.

But the death of the Bird of the Sun is not forever. In the ashes there remains a small whitish worm, which grows and *develops until, on the third day, a new phoenix arises on strong young wings. Reverently, the bird gathers up ashes of its sire, or former self, and sets off westward. A long journey later, the flight ends at the sacred Egyptian city of On-Heliopolis. There, on the altar of the sun, the appropriate funeral rites are celebrated by the priest, and then the young, the only phoenix sets out again for his ancestral home in paradise. On this return journey, he is accompanied by all the birds of this world, his mortal cousins — the eagle and the goose, the hawk and the sparrow fly side by side without fear until it is time to turn back at the borders of the immortal county. From that point, the phoenix flies on alone, not to reappear for another half-millennium of human history. Then again he will bring a year of good fortune, of peace for the righteous and death to tyrants.*[3]

Death and resurrection. Dying and renewal. These are rhythms of life that are as deeply ingrained in our consciousness as they are perennial in our mythology. Constantly, this rhythm is repeated. We see this in stages of physical development as a child moves from infancy to childhood and from childhood to adolescence and on to the various stages of adulthood. In terms of psychological development, the same holds true: the worlds we construct out of our experience at one stage of life cease to exist as we mature, and we many times can change the way we make sense of things. At every turn, something passes away and something else comes into view.

All around us, things are passing away. Glorious nature in full bloom marches steadily toward the next winter's death. And the next spring. When we find and acknowledge this rhythm in our own lives, we come into harmony with the greater rhythms around us: the passing of time, the changing of the seasons, the cycles of the tides and the moon. Although the cycles involve suffering and loss, the result is not a narrowing of life. Quite the contrary, it is an expansion, a growth into new life. By opening out the boundaries that we have placed upon our experience through out-moded ideas or beliefs, we make room for a fuller experience in and of the world. We begin to catch sight of something at once strange and familiar: life as it is.

For what is dying is *a way of seeing oneself and the world* that has outlasted its usefulness. In fact, it is the death of failure itself. Once an individual has passed through the experience of failure and has come into new life on the other side, it is no longer possible to believe in failure in quite the same way again. While similar events may occur, the setbacks and losses are now seen in a different light: not as failure that is an end in itself, but a failing that leads beyond itself to a more fully lived life.

The phoenix of myth — and interestingly it's a myth that appears in several cultures of the world, suggesting the apparent universality of its meaning — sees death coming and chooses to accept it, even to embrace it. The bird has no mind to compare with the human mind; what it knows it just knows. Out of the ashes on its funeral pyre arises a new bird, even more colorful than the one that died. We can't help but sense that the newly found color in its rejuvenated, resurrected wings has something to do with the former bird's *acceptance* of death. For the born-again phoenix, the rewards of this acceptance are hidden no more.

SECOND EXERCISE

Think back on a failure experience that was important to you. It may be something you're involved with now, but if you are in the midst of a very confusing or painful active experience of failure, look back instead on an earlier experience that you've had some time to come to terms with.

Close your eyes for a moment and allow the memory of the failure experience you've chosen to become vivid to you. Try to remember what you were like, who was there, what happened, and how you felt. Take time with this.

A. Describe the experience in as much detail as you can.

B. In the course of this experience, how were the important areas of your life affected? Think about the impact on your work, your role in the community, and on your intimate and family relationships. Reflect on any changes in your personal habits and in your emotions.

C. What role did your personal strengths and resources play at this time, or were they unavailable to you?

D. Now that you have recalled the experience to mind and heart, what significance does it have for you today? What themes or questions emerged from it? How do you see this experience in relation to the rest of your life?

THREE COMMON AREAS
for FAILURE
School, Work, Relationships

*Every creator painfully experiences the chasm between his inner
vision and its ultimate expression.*

ISAAC BASHEVIS SINGER

*The easiest kind of relationship for me is with ten thousand people.
The hardest is with one.*

JOAN BAEZ

THIS IS A CHAPTER OF VOICES. As we explore the experience of
failure, the accounts of others whose journeys may in some
aspects resemble our own can offer encouragement and
inspiration. As these stories demonstrate, failure is not a
simple event. Its antecedents may extend far back into a
person's history. The crisis itself impinges radically on the
present, and the future, once a comfortable extension of
the present, now lies open to possibility and surprise. Of
course, the stories also make clear that failure is painful
and distressing, causing difficult reorientation and a

97

sweeping reassessment of many things that had always been taken for granted.

Because failure occurs across the whole spectrum of individual growth and development, and because most of life involves simultaneous combinations of interior and exterior experience, it is admittedly somewhat artificial to define the types of failure simply on the basis of "locale." Wherever it first occurs, any significant crisis reverberates through the individual's experience: intrapsychic, interpersonal and in all the "outside" circumstances of life (school, job, and the like). Nevertheless, it can be helpful at times to propose abstract categorizations for the sake of discussion. In this spirit we will examine failure stories from three areas that are common to most people's experience: School, Work, and Key Relationships.

FAILURE IN THE EXTERNAL LIFE: SCHOOL

The purpose of education is to show a person how to define himself authentically and spontaneously in relation to his world.

THOMAS MERTON

School can provide an environment for authentic personal and interpersonal development. This is the ideal. Sometimes, however, school is also the place where individuals, buffeted by the conflicting voices of overbearing mentors, critical classmates, and confusing cultural norms, can actually lose their sense of individual identity. The story that follows is a case in point. Here, Anne, following the suggestions of others, gradually loses touch with herself and her direction. Accustomed to success in school, an abrupt confrontation with failure brought her to an awareness of her personal alienation. From this point — but only after getting to this point — she was able to begin the process of transformation and growth.

ANNE'S STORY

Businesslike, yet warm, Anne projects calm self-confidence. At 43, she feels she is now entering her most productive period of life, yet for years she was near suicide. Her story is one of discovering her own voice and her own path and of the price she paid for this knowledge.

"I grew up at a time and in a home that really honored education. Education in the 1950s, with the postwar baby boom going on, was really important. And my mother put a lot of value on education, even serving on the school board. So I really went along with the idea of school being a big part of life. Success in school equalled success in life, in my eyes.

"I sailed through school with ease, ending up at the top of my class at high school graduation. At the encouragement of my choir director, I had been studying piano with his teacher. I had a history of latching onto teacher figures and doing what they wanted me to do. I was encouraged by people I admired to go into music, and I did. I moved from a small suburban town to a major city university to study for a bachelor's of music in piano, planning on becoming a professional pianist. While I was there, it started to dawn on me that although I had been good when I was in a small town, in this big environment there were people who were clearly more talented, but I truly enjoyed it and so I continued. I liked the life of being a student. It was very involving — you ate, slept, breathed music at least 24 hours a day, and so it was very fulfilling. By the time I got out, I knew I didn't have the stuff to be a successful professional pianist, so I decided that the next logical move would be to go into the scholarly study of music and become a music professor! You know, here I was in the university; it seemed the obvious thing to do — combine my love of school with my love of music. Again I met someone who encouraged me to go to his school, and because I admired him, and was interested in his work, I aligned myself with him. Now I found myself in graduate school, having basically followed other people's suggestions about what to do next. I remember a scholar who came to do guest lectures on musicology. He said, 'What a musicologist needs is *sitzfleisch* — meaning, meat on your rear end for sitting for hours at the library. When I heard that I was alarmed — that didn't sound like what I wanted. Yet, I really didn't feel I had any alternatives. All I had ever known was school, and I didn't know myself well enough to be able to imagine other directions I could take.

"Just two months before I was to graduate with my master's degree, a professor with whom I was in a relationship decided to leave the school and move away. As was my custom, I followed him. I had completed all my coursework requirements; I had finished one thesis project and just had the second to wrap up, yet I dropped out. In every single class I had taken during all these years of schooling, I had graduated first. My entire school career had been a history of grand and towering success. But in this case, I didn't want to continue. The work I had to do in order to finish the second thesis project seemed overwhelming, my lover had left, and I didn't want my master's degree — it felt like another nail in the coffin — 'Oh, now you've got your master's, time for a Ph.D!' It was becoming more and more clear that I wasn't sure if I wanted to be in academia, and I didn't even know if I wanted to be in music! I dropped out.

"This was the first time I had embarked on a course of study and failed. The result was I shut down. I followed Richard to a small town in the boonies, where he wanted to settle, and stayed behind after we broke up. I was very alone and it was very tough. I felt shame at spending my parents' money on college and not getting anything out of it. I felt ashamed of the way my life had gone, of the waste it seemed to be. What I really felt the most was no feeling — I wasn't who I thought I was, and I didn't know who I was. I couldn't tell what decisions had been my own or those that had been influenced by others. I felt that anything I touched I would taint, so it would be better for me stay away from than to be with other people — and maybe, best of all, if I completely disappeared.

"So I was living in a tiny house way up north, not functioning much, not seeing anyone, and I became full of despair and physically ill. It was that kind of despair that is flat affect — where you could easily be run down by a car because you wouldn't move. But I couldn't even get it up to kill myself. At my lowest, in the dead of winter, I just allowed the fire in the wood stove to go out. That was the only source of heat. I expected to freeze, but I discovered that some small kernel of will to live was left in me. Instead, I went to stay with my sister for a while. And when you find that you haven't killed yourself, that there's some little spark left in you, then that allows you to move out of the depths just a little bit.

"A change of scene slowly pulled me out of the depression — and there were little decisions I could make for myself that would give me some clues about myself. The lack of wood fire made me cold, so I moved. It was little steps, little decisions, checking in with myself as I went. Later, I had to move out of my apartment into a new one, and was able to discern that I had liked the first one better, and maybe I should try to find something like it. Before, because I had placed so much authority in school and others, I lacked the objectivity and I lacked the connection with my feelings — I had been so depressed and alienated from myself that I couldn't tell. Then later, when I tried a job and it didn't work out, I could say to myself, 'Looks to me like I shouldn't be doing this.' It became a process of observing myself and reading the signs, saying, 'Well, I guess that wasn't it. It was a good shot but let's try something different.'

"It was a long, long road back from that time when I was ready to die. But the realization that what you had thought of your life was not the way it was — figuring that out, and coming to integration with that takes years. And I had to learn to discern my voice from the voices of others. Sometimes I had followed others blindly, but at times in my life history I must have had some of my own will involved in the moves I had made. But how could I tell what was me and what was them? It just took time and patience. It was a good six years after dropping out of school that I began to make moves out of a sense of my own direction. Now, almost 20 years since I was at my depths, I know myself very well. For example, I'm very in tune with my body. Right now, we've been talking for awhile and I feel that my throat is dry and pretty soon I'll have to stop, or get some water. Or, when I get an uncomfortable tightness in my chest, I acknowledge it as a signal that I'm feeling pressure about something, and I investigate. I simply know myself better.

"Now, I find myself doing work that uses a lot of my interests and abilities, but not in a way I could have foreseen. And I think my route to this job is typical of how I have learned to gather information about myself. I spent some time with career counselors when I was ready to make a change. They use a process in which you identify personal traits and passions and dreams and abilities and then help you translate these into job ideas. After going through this process, I knew the kind of work I wanted, where I wanted to be, the kind of organization I was interested in, all of that. When this job was advertised in the paper, it virtually had my name on it! I knew it would be a good choice for me. I went into the interview carrying the job description I had envisioned and written up, and it matched beautifully. I'm in charge of producing adult education programs within a non-profit organization. This uses my producing interests, my teaching ability, and lately has even incorporated my interest in musicology.

"It took me a long time to learn how to trust myself. And I know that I will never feel the kind of failure that I've felt ever again, and that's good. Some people make their marks early in life, and then head downhill. For me, it's been a long, slow climb, but I feel as if I'm finally coming into my power."

Anne's story illustrates how one can use the experience of failure as the starting point for meaningful growth.

School had been her universe, her context for understanding. When school life let her down and no longer seemed to satisfy her image of her life, failure brought her back to herself.

For many students, school is a problematic environment. This fact is commented on by people both outside and inside the education field. In a recent interview published in *The Boston Globe*, author and educational innovator Theodore Sizer criticizes prevailing models for schooling that are based upon obsolete forms of industrial organization. "The present design of American schools is still based on the 19th-century model of the factory. You parade a kid through the assembly line, slapping on various parts: History is the fender, French is the steering wheel. . . . none of the parts is related, and at the end, he gets a certificate of completion, which in our system has nothing to do with proven competence, but is a sort of secular rite of passage." Sizer goes on to say that the "batch processing" of students requiring that "all students should be taught the same things at the same age and in the same way virtually guarantees the incompetence of many students."[1]

With the decline of liberal education in our colleges and universities in this century, the purpose of education has shifted from the cultivation of the innate talents of individual students to the preparation of a managerial elite. This was not the ideal of classical education and indeed the etymology of the word education (to lead out) implies a process that begins with the student, not with the society. The "liberal" in "liberal education," by the way, has nothing to do with political liberalism (as in the Democratic Party or socialism). It means "liberating," freeing up the mind from prejudice and misinformation so as to think clearly and act independently. In Anne's story of failure we see someone whose education neither liberated her mind or led her effectively out into the world; instead it (the people who taught her, the curriculum itself) reinforced in her personality what was probably a preexisting tendency toward dependency and inauthenticity (living her life according to other people's values and beliefs). Nowadays there is a pervasive view of school as a sort of boot camp for life. The well-known phrase "the battle of Waterloo was won on the playing fields of Eton" has a quaint historical appeal but is probably more true than ever, even though today's battles are more commonly waged in the corporate boardroom.

The idea that school is a preparatory microcosm for "the real world" is a damaging and dangerous distortion of the ideals of education. Especially if one believes that this world is already overfilled with adults who are themselves neurotic, misguided, anxious and unhappy, why on earth should we be preparing anyone for that? There was recently an advertisement for an educational service that turned a home computer into a powerful on-line teaching aid. The ad contained a photograph showing a young boy, about six or seven, seated at the keyboard and staring into the monitor. Underneath, the caption read in bold type: "Little Johnny is getting ready for graduate school." My blood ran cold. Robbing a child of childhood, for the sake of some imagined benefit to be harvested somewhere in an incomprehensible future, is to arrive at misery by the shortest possible route.

School should first and foremost be a safe place, where young people can acquire and develop skills, benefit from the exchange of ideas, broaden their horizons and fail. School should provide a context where one can "fail early and fail often," by taking risks that stretch one's abilities. Fortunately, most of us encounter at one point or another a teacher who has the gift of knowing just how to blend discipline and encouragement. Such a teacher knows how to establish a framework in which a student can safely try something new. In such a framework, failure can contribute to learning, instead of inhibiting the attempt.

Slowly, some schools are waking up to the need to explore the dynamics of both success and failure in learning. Some subjects seem more amenable to this process. For example, at a university in Texas, senior level engineering students take a required course whose informal title is "Failure 101." In this course, students discover the breadth of their own creativity as they purposefully look for the "wrong" ways of doing things. They are following a rich scientific tradition; in fact, many of the world's greatest inventions came out of the spirit of exploration in which all results are welcomed, without judgment, as further steps along the path. It is said that Thomas Edison explained, after many unsuccessful attempts at one of his creations, "I have simply invented 1,000 ways not to design a lightbulb."

Creative expression, whether in science or in art, thrives on failure: on an approach that embraces all outcomes as useful. However, even in the arts where so many have succeeded precisely because they took creative risks, the willingness to dare and to fail can be dampened or extinguished.

JENNIFER'S STORY

Far better it is to dare mighty things, to win glorious triumphs even though checkered by failure, than to rank with those poor spirits who neither enjoy nor suffer much because they live in the gray twilight that knows neither victory nor defeat.

THEODORE ROOSEVELT

"When I was growing up, I felt very strongly that I wanted to be an actor. After I finished high school, I applied to the best acting schools I knew about, and after a number of auditions was fortunate to win a place in a class of only 18 students the following fall.

"In this school, we had a great deal of technical training — movement, speech, theater production, everything. We also had acting classes, and at the end of each term our class would mount a production — it might be a series of scenes or an entire play. We worked so hard on this production — not only because we wanted to do well, but I remember how much we cared about what everybody else thought — our instructors, the students who were at higher levels, even students who were more junior than we were. We were so aware of needing to do well that often the rehearsals were not very enjoyable, and few people really risked using the rehearsal time for exploration. At the end of the term, our evaluations would be weighted heavily by our 'success' in the performance. So everything would go into this 'live or die' experience. I remember doing a merely workmanlike job with my roles in spite of the incredible effort I put into them, and then dragging myself back to my parents' home at the end of the term to recuperate before the next term started.

"I spent two years in this program, and decided that I just wasn't a great fit. Besides, I was dying to travel, and I knew that there was good theater training to be had in England. Again I went through the audition process, but this time I ended up in a small one-year program on the outskirts of London. This wasn't a mainstream theater school, but for my needs it was the perfect one. Instead of the twice-a-year performance schedule of my old school, we were in either rehearsal or performance continuously. In ten months each student did ten plays. And we were goaded, cajoled, embarrassed, and inspired into going 'over the top.' Rehearsals were to be energetically used for exploration, and nothing was 'wrong.' The only way to fail was to fail to dare. And so I, and the other students, stretched beyond the old comfort zones into marvelous, crazy, surprising, sensitive, emotional performances. It was a wonderful lesson in what happens when the concept of 'failure' is removed from the vocabulary, and when creative expression and the right to dare are given authority."

Jennifer's story reminds us of the statement by President Theodore Roosevelt at the beginning of this section.

Sadly, the authority, the permission to fail creatively that Jennifer's story highlights, is rarely given in school. Often, the pressure to succeed is as great as it is in the most competitive business environments. Furthermore, pressure is not confined to the time a child actually spends in the classroom: home and family life are drawn into the vortex, with parents urging their children to greater and greater achievement in academics, in athletics, in any area where achievement is possible. What is the result? We like to believe that people learn from their experience. They also may be captive to their experience. If a child is trained to see life itself as a competition where participants are divided into leagues of winners and losers, then that child will grow into an adult who sees the world as a grown-up version of the same thing. This does not make winning any sweeter (and such winners usually lack empathy for their adversaries), nor does it make failure any easier to cope with. It may be impossible for such a person to see failure as a positive resource.

FAILURE IN THE EXTERNAL LIFE: WORK

Sigmund Freud maintained that love and work were the two basic needs of all adults. The famous Viennese psychiatrist Viktor Frankl, who founded an entire school of psychotherapy on the understanding that the "drive to meaning" is a fundamental human need, gives work an important place in an individual's well-being. When work is denied or impossible, the negative effects on an individual can be clinically described and assessed.

The meaning of life, we have said, is not to be questioned but to be responded to, for we are responsible to life. It follows from this that the response should not be given in words, but in acting, by doing. Moreover, the correct response depends upon the situation and the person in all his concreteness. The response, so to speak, must have incorporated that concreteness into itself. The right response will therefore be an active response within the actual conditions of everyday living, within the area of human responsibility.

The existential importance of work is most clearly seen where work is entirely eliminated from a person's life, as in unemployment. Psychological studies of the unemployed have arrived at the concept of unemployment neurosis. Remarkably enough, the most prominent symptom of this neurosis is not depression, but apathy. The unemployed become increasingly indifferent and their initiative more and more trickles away. This apathy is not without grave dangers. It makes people incapable of grasping the helping hand which may be extended to them. [2]

On an individual basis failure at a job can have a devastating effect on a person's self-esteem. Over the course of a career, men and women come to identify themselves with their work. Expressions in our ordinary conversation such as "She lives for her job" or "He's been eating, breathing, and sleeping that assignment ever since he came on board" illustrate the extent to which this is true. Naturally, if one wishes to succeed at any endeavor, commitment is necessary. But there is a level of involvement which goes beyond commitment to enmeshment. That sense of balance, which is so critical in the sorting out of one's values and priorities, disappears, and life takes on an oddly misshapen quality. Recently, we were told of one individual whose self-esteem was so entirely wrapped up in his career that after losing his job, he was unable to admit this failure even to members of his own family. Every morning he would wake up at his usual time, get dressed for the office, go down to the station and ride his usual train into town. Once there he would go to the public library and remain there all day until it was time to take the commuter home. This went on for months before he was able to overcome his denial and begin to come to terms with his situation.

As people become enmeshed in their work, they begin to lose interest in outside activities; their circle of relationships begins to shrink. This can be dangerous, for both activities and relationships not only serve to advance the quality of life when things are going well, they are necessary and healing supports when things fall apart.

That life should be balanced is such a truism that many forget about it entirely. Driven by the pressures placed upon them by work or family and by the expectations of their peer group, men and women begin to let that balance waver. Failure, once it hits, finds an easy mark in people whose commitments to work have caused them to sacrifice the very resources — individual and social — that would have enabled them to keep their equilibrium.

We have already listened to the story of Jim, the advertising executive (in Chapter 2). Here is another story about failure in work, this time from a working artist. The stakes, though different, feel just as high.

JUDY'S STORY

Judy has been in front of the spotlights, in one way or another, since she was a young girl. Now 35, she has been a successful dancer, musical theater performer, and stage actress. She is a vivacious, lithe, attractive woman. Last year she won her first major role in a film. She describes a failure experience that served as a catalyst, moving her out of the world of performing into the exciting new realm of producing.

> "I came from a very high-achieving family, workaholic parents, both of them. In our family, success meant going for 100% — not 89%, not 91%, we were to always aim for 100%. That taught me (unfortunately) to toe the line — not make waves and not think for myself. It also made me extremely competitive, which I still am. There are pros and cons to that — you need to be able to accept yourself if you fail, yet still have the spirit to keep going.
>
> "Luckily I did well in school. In our family there was incredible pressure to succeed, and I felt that the siblings in my family who didn't 'measure up' were treated worse than the others — nagged, torn down, made to feel stupid. So it was very important to succeed — failure was not accepted, it was incomprehensible.
>
> "My career started in my early teens, when I joined a young professional performing troupe. My teens were a real blossoming time for me — I could

see that I was good at this, and I loved the excitement. I pretty much did hit that 100% goal in my teens — I was also good at academics. By the end of high school I knew I wanted to go into the performing arts, and I went to a college that had a highly-regarded professional theater training program. And my career has been successful by most standards — I was able to make a living by acting, I have worked with many fine companies, and I've had some good roles. In my view, I feel I've had an adequate career but haven't really excelled.

"There is an inherent fear of failure in the acting profession. By its nature the field is 'me' oriented — you're always having to think about yourself — you are, in fact, the 'instrument.' So actors are extremely self-absorbed. How do I look? How do I sound? How am I moving? And it's a very competitive profession in which you're always having to prove your worth — every time you finish a play, it's time to look for a new job.

"The only time I was ever fired from a job, I realized how important it had been for me to be accepted. I saw it coming. I was hired over the phone on the basis of a recommendation to do a show out of town. It was a two-hander — just two characters in the play. The other actor was someone I admired greatly and had never worked with — I was awed and thrilled to be working with him. We met to rehearse, and the director was this very flamboyant personality, a passionate type. We spent two days around the table. It was going exceedingly well; I was getting a strong sense of the character and the director was in love with me. The next day we left the table and began to work on our feet. I often start out self-consciously;

I'm worried I won't be good enough and just can't dive in full steam. So I started out sitting on a chair and making notes in the script with a pencil while we worked through the play. All of a sudden things were different. The director was on me for every gesture, every line. Nothing was right. It was a disastrous day. I think he was in a panic because he didn't know me, couldn't trust that I'd come through with the performance he wanted in the short rehearsal period, and it was a project he really cared about. I went home and cried. The next day it was still a disaster. He informed me he was already looking for a replacement. I didn't fight. I just went along with it, and said, 'If you feel you made a mistake, pull me now.' I gave up.

"I was devastated. The other actor had been functioning brilliantly, which only made my situation worse. I felt powerless, stupid, self-conscious, untalented and worthless. It was as though what I had always feared was actually true — that I couldn't act, that I had always been a sham.

"I dealt with it first by withdrawing. You put a shell around you, to prove that you're not really being touched. I wouldn't cry, I wouldn't scream. I tried to retain control of myself — maybe because what was most painful was that I didn't have control of the situation.

"I couldn't eat. I felt as though everything was happening in fast-forward. I threw myself into exercising — became compulsive for a few weeks, trying to force myself to feel better by looking good. Luckily, my friends and family were supportive, and they got me through it. The change was gradual. Eventually I was able to stop justifying myself and laying blame on the director, and I could just accept that some things work out, some don't. All I can do is my best. Failure has eased the pressure I put on myself.

"Professionally, this event was a real turning point for me. If I had responded differently, I might have managed to keep that job. It was a job to kill for. I used to fight all the time — but I was entering a point in my life, at 32, when I just thought I don't need this anymore. Ultimately, I wasn't willing to put myself on an emotional roller coaster in order to keep this job. I had been noticing more and more that I no longer had the all-consuming passion to act that others did. But this incident compounded a lot of the concerns I had about acting, and the actor's life. And I was beginning to think about settling down, having a family, maybe expanding into some new directions. So actually this experience turned out to be a catalyst.

"For at least five years now, I've been interested in producing. Since this event, I haven't totally left acting, but I've been pursuing producing much more vigorously. I have a project now that we're trying to get funded, and I hope it goes. I'm also helping to organize a major artists conference, which is a different kind of producing. I think I would have gotten around to this eventually, but this failure experience moved me toward it much more quickly. I've found that I miss the acclaim that you get from being on stage, but I can find support and affirmation from other sources — close friends, my boyfriend, other work that I'm doing. And I know now that I can be loved just for who I am.

"Failure isn't a final ultimate horrible thing. It means not achieving a goal, and that's not necessarily a negative thing. To me, failure is an experience, just as success is, just as life is. You learn, you reassess, and then you keep going. Acting was once a passion. Now it seems to be a fond avocation, and I'm on to new things."

FAILURE WHERE THE INTERNAL AND EXTERNAL WORLDS MEET: MARRIAGE & FAMILY LIFE

Seldom or never does a marriage develop into an individual relationship smoothly and without crisis. There is no birth of consciousness without pain.

C. G. JUNG

An area in which many people we interviewed described a tremendous amount of pain and struggle was in failed relationships. Perhaps because failure in a relationship may be interpreted as a shortcoming in one's own being, the sting seems sharper. People wrote and spoke with us about how they reacted to a relationship that ended, and of how they came to understand the experience. One woman explained, "After my marriage failed, I felt terrible because I loved the man and I thought my children needed him. The story of how we all survived and made a go of it would take many pages to tell. But I learned about myself, about courage, about risk, about love. Now I simply feel that marriage took a different path than I had anticipated — so did my family." Yet although this topic can be difficult to approach, humor was present as well. A 74-year-old man noted, "I've had a very rich life, but I've had to pay for it, too. I'm on my fourth marriage now, which means I've had to buy back my grave plot three times so far. It's a shame; I wanted those first two so much because they had such a nice view."

We are just as capable of failing and learning from our experience in marriage and family life and other key relationships as in school or at work. Indeed, since the Industrial Revolution, the nuclear family has become increasingly an endangered species and the failure of traditional neighborhoods and communities is given as a leading factor in the rising violence in our cities. Perhaps in no other area of life are the rewards of transforming failure as great as they are in the family. Conversely, the danger posed by a refusal to attend to family difficulties is equally great. This is due simply to the importance of the contribution that intimate relationships make to the meaningfulness of an individual's life. Intimate family or familylike relationships can serve either as obstacles or opportunities for any individual's growth into authenticity, into true self-knowledge, with integrity towards his or her *own* principles. In the following story, we will follow an exploration of both obstacle and opportunity.

JULIA'S STORY

Julia, a striking woman in her early 40s, speaks and listens with thoughtful intensity. She expresses her tastes and personality in everything she touches — ranging from her artwork, to the colorful clothing she chooses, to the music with which she surrounds herself. At the root of this self-expression is a self-knowledge that has been hard won.

> "I grew up in a small Southwestern town, a very rural area. I was the third child of four in a ranching family, living in a place where all the people were church-going, community people. My two older siblings were boys, and as far as my family was concerned, they were 'it.' Even to me, they were the authority. What I said, thought or did was clearly sec-

ondary since the main purpose for my life was to grow up to get married.

"Just about everybody in our town was related to each other, and everyone was married, or almost everyone. Not only was everyone married, but everyone stayed married; divorce was practically unheard of in the time of my childhood. I grew up with the idea that marriage works, that marriage is forever. The marriage vows were something that I fantasized about a lot as a child. People got married 'to have and to hold, from this day forward, for better or worse, for richer, for poorer, in sickness and in health, till death us do part,' and there was just no other way about it in my mind.

"So as I grew older and became involved in relationships, I naturally equated marriage with happiness. I remember having a serious boyfriend when I was in the seventh grade. He was a sophomore, so it was a big deal because of the difference in our ages. We would often fantasize about our marriage, which would take place immediately after high school, creating names for our children, dreaming about our home. I had several serious relationships during my high school years; in fact, I would usually think that something was wrong if I wasn't seriously involved with someone! These were nightmarish years for my parents because I was always breaking curfews, staying out until all hours of the morning, but always, from my point of view, doing what I needed to do, which was being 'in relationship' with someone.

"Although I wasn't particularly encouraged to excel at school, I actually became something of a legend in high school. I got good grades, but I also managed to do all the other things — I was a cheerleader, class valedictorian, editor of the newspaper, won awards for acting in school plays; I was even homecoming queen. I was popular and successful, kind of on top of the world. But it never occurred to my parents, or to me, that I should do anything other than plan for marriage. I did choose a career, but it was in one of the traditional 'women's fields' and it was clearly just to 'fall back on' in case something happened to my husband.

"I knew my husband in high school. He was older than I, and it wasn't until I was a senior and he was in college that we actually dated. I was very attracted to him because he was different from most of my other boyfriends — he seemed to be more self-confident and self-directed. He was also very playful and outgoing, fun to be with. I ended up going to the college that he attended. From almost the first day that I set foot on campus, we became a 'number.' Although I was involved in a lot of extra-curricular activities my freshman year, slowly they all sort of fell away. All I really wanted to do was be with Glen. I totally gave myself over to him, and let my other relationships and interests fall away.

"Glen was really special to me from the very beginning. He introduced me to a lot of ideas and ways of thinking I'd never been exposed to before, and I admired his intelligence and cool demeanor. I settled quite easily into the position of being the 'low one' in the relationship, which was just as I knew it was supposed to be. We married after my sophomore year of college, right after Glen graduated. I felt like it was the perfect beginning to the perfect match.

"I was looking forward to a storybook marriage. In my family, my parents never disagreed, at least not in front of us, and I believed that because we were such a perfect couple, we would always be happy and would live out this incredibly harmonious life. Quickly, reality set in. On our honeymoon, I remember being terribly upset over the fact that we liked different dressings on our salads! I couldn't accept the discovery that we might have differences. Since I didn't know how to deal with them, and neither did Glen, I began early on to deny them and thus, to deny myself. Not only did I withdraw from confrontation or discussion, but I began to assume that I was wrong. After all, if Glen thought something, then it must be Truth, it must be right. I knew from my childhood that 'girls don't know' or that what they know doesn't really matter. So I gave him the place of authority and all-knowing in our marriage and in my life. Yet, I didn't give this authority over willingly, because over the years a lot of resentment and anger built up between us over all kinds of issues that we never dealt with.

"Having children compounded the friction in our relationship. After the birth of our daughter, we quickly lost whatever sense of closeness we'd had. He was distracted by increasing hours and pressures at work, and I was feeling trapped at home and was unable to share my feelings with him, partly because I felt I wasn't 'supposed' to have them. When our daughter was three we had a second child, a son, who was a difficult baby, just as I had been as a child. We struggled along for several years, playing at being the perfect family. Glen had enough problems at work, so he was unavailable to me, and I felt that I had failed to be the happy and loving wife and mother that I knew I should be. By this time I had given up trying to communicate who I really was to him (if in fact I knew!) and he wasn't asking. I remember nights of lying in bed listening to him go on about his day at work, and feeling that I was doing what I was supposed to do: listen. Then, he'd say, 'So, how are you?' and I'd just say, 'fine' and turn away. I was so far from being myself that I don't know if I could have put into words what was wrong. We were two miserable human beings, locked up from each other, unable to speak or to listen to each other, unaware of how to even go about beginning to communicate with each other! I felt stuck, and without any options for movement. But still I insisted to myself that this was what marriage was all about — I assumed this was what they meant by 'for better or for worse.'

"I began to have problems in my relationship with my son, and we were at a loss as to what to do. He was willful and determined, the kind of kid who would do exactly what I told him not to do, and I was very frustrated at not knowing how to deal with him. A light bulb went off for me, finally, when a close friend remarked after witnessing a scene between the two of us, 'Wow! It seems that this boy was given to you, Julia, to help you work through something in your life.' That was the beginning, for me, of viewing life as an opportunity. Another friend around this time also told me to consider that children are never 'wrong,' they just are. I began to see that I was trying to make this child into something that I wanted him to be, and that I was missing who he really was. Slowly I began to make the connection — that I had been, for at least ten years now, trying to make myself into the person I thought I should be. And we were all missing out.

"It was just as this realization was dawning that we were visited by someone we'd known from our school days who happened to be traveling in the area. We invited Luke to dinner, looking forward to seeing him because he had always been an interesting character. We finished dinner and talked into the early hours of the morning, mostly about Glen's work. From the beginning I was intrigued by the way this person talked, the words he used, the ideas he presented. It was as if my own words and ideas were being expressed right out of his mouth. It was a very strange and yet soothing sensation. For someone who hadn't been in the practice of expressing her own ideas or emotions for a long time, this felt exceptional. I also sensed that this man respected me as a woman, that he appreciated my thoughts and ideas in a way that I hadn't felt in a long time. About a month later he was back in town and we decided that he would stay with us again. He arrived in the early afternoon; I was alone at home. We sat at the kitchen table. After the usual small talk he suddenly turned to me and asked, 'And how are you?' He said it in such a way that I felt totally held by his caring concern, and I broke down and started to cry. After that I spoke with him openly; I felt I had permission to be myself. I had never met a man who was so interested in the very things I had longed to share with someone about life. He truly listened to me until I felt renewed.

"We spent a lot of playful time together, and by the end of his visit I realized that something very amazing was happening — that I was beginning to fall in love with him. This was a very scary thing. After all, I was a happily married woman with two children and a dog and a home in a community that knew me to be a solid, respectable woman. The only right thing to do would be to deny this experience, to snuff it out and pretend that it never existed, just as I had denied all other feelings or thoughts that had come to me that didn't seem to fit. But I knew that I could never deny this. It was too clear, too strong, too much 'me' to be denied.

"He went away again and I went through a week in which I was operating as if I were in a dream. Nothing felt real, I was a spectator in my own life. I lost whole chunks of time. It was as if I had been picked up from my world, shaken around and spit back out, with a demand to make sense of it all from this dizzying perspective. I felt a deep sense of failure and of alienation from everything and everyone around me. Eventually, I realized that I had to tell someone what I was experiencing. I decided to call Luke. I had to check whether I was totally off base, or whether he felt anything like what I was feeling. I called him and told him I thought I was falling in love with him.

"The days and weeks that followed were obviously very difficult to comprehend. I acted in ways that I had never acted before, unwilling to deny any feeling, thought or experience that came to me, seemingly driven to play this scene out to discover what lay beneath it all. I was amazed at my own sense of courage and clarity as I defined myself more and more in relation to the experience with Luke. My conversations with him were like conversations with myself, a new and exciting me that I had lost touch with or never bothered to get to know. There was a feeling of recalling ideas and concepts that I had really always known but had repressed over the years. I felt energy and vitality and a sense of direction that was all new for me. The only problem, of course, was that I was married to someone else, and none of this fit with who I had been just days before.

"Through this drastic change in my life, I gained some clarity on my marriage, and finally was able to recognize how dysfunctional it was. And yet I still felt a deep commitment to the marriage and to our children. I told Glen that our marriage was in trouble, and I told him about Luke. Of course, this was an extremely difficult time for us, and many marriages would have broken up right here. But strangely enough, our marriage didn't dissolve. In fact, we became more engaged with each other than we had been in years, although it was mainly negative energy that was flowing between us at first. We stayed up for hours talking and arguing into the night, but at least we were communicating. And I was no longer willing to avoid dealing with disagreements. This was the biggest one of our marriage, and we confronted it with anger, fear, and honesty.

"Glen and I went into therapy, which helped us tremendously in our efforts to sort through all that had happened to us to get us to the point of Luke's impact. We went way back to our childhood days and our parent's models for marriage, to our own early marriage days, working our way up through the births of our children, through the crises in Glen's work life, and through our lack of real communication during all of it. We realized that somehow the trust had broken down between us. We began to like each other again.

"Much has happened since this point, and we certainly haven't come to any final, resting point in our relationship, and I hope we never do. I can see now that for a marriage to really work, it takes a constant commitment to examine ourselves and the relationship and all that we each bring to it. For all the positive work we've done in our relationship, Glen and I still confront each other periodically with the idea of divorce, and I continue to struggle with a desire to include Luke in my life. But, clearly, this event — for all the pain and upheaval it has caused — has had a tremendously positive effect on how I see myself and my life. Through my experience with Luke, I've been reawakened to myself and have a new commitment to be authentic in all my relationships. This is a far cry from the girl who learned never to speak, only to listen.

"As I have become more truly myself, Glen has become more truly himself. I came to realize that he was never who he had been playing at, either. Those nights when we lay in bed as he told me all about work? — he was just doing what he thought he was supposed to do. In fact, there was always this deep fear on his part that if he would tell someone who he really was, they would leave or would think less of him. He needed to learn how to share who he really is just as much as I did. I feel that he, too, has gone through a miraculous change, and is now willing to fully participate in our growth as a couple.

"My relationship with both my kids is so much better. I am able to be much more available to them, and I have become a real advocate of encouraging children to speak their own thoughts, and to make sure they know that even if we don't agree with them, we will accept them and their ideas. A big part of my role as a mother is making sure that our children are heard. Over the course of the years of therapy I also went back to school, and took up studies that led me to discover a whole aspect of my vocation that had been hidden. I've just completed my work toward the degree, and I'm looking to the future with a lot of hope and excitement. I feel that now I am a totally different person from the woman who subjugated herself to some false ideal of 'wife and mother.' Although old parts of myself keep coming up — self-doubts, worries that I'm not smart enough, not talented enough — I know that I have what it takes, and that my voice, my ideas count."

Julia's story is particularly useful in the way it demonstrates the relativity of the meanings of failure and success. Her marriage looked to most people on the outside as though it were a success, for after all it corresponded neatly in form and content to most other marriages in the community, and the prevailing assumption was that the community norm should be the individual's norm as well. From inside the marriage, the relationship looked to her as though it had become a failure because of the lack of communication and warmth between the partners. From the outside, and even from within the marriage — on Glen's side of it — Julia's friendship with Luke must have looked like a breach of faith, a self-indulgent escapade: a failure on some level. From Julia's viewpoint, Luke appeared as a liberating angel, who, upsetting though his presence was, nonetheless brought good news of benefit, ultimately, to everyone in the family. Luke brought Julia to the door of successful psychological growth; on her own she stepped through it into a far better time. Who is to say what is failure, what is success in such a story? It is often too easy for us to pass judgment on other people's lives when, if we are honest with ourselves, we would acknowledge that our own story is also one fraught with tensions, paradoxes and as yet unrecognized problems and opportunities.

As Julia's story demonstrates, even experiences of failure that cause great disruption and unhappiness in relationships can bestow important rewards. This is not to say that the rewards she discovered could not have come to her in any other way. Rather, the unfolding story of her life, with all the victories and defeats, all the challenges to her growth and integrity that had to be dealt with in one way or another, carried her to a decisive moment. The part of her that had for so long remained imprisoned in her own limited self-awareness, broke free. The consequences of this long delayed liberation have a quality of both anarchy and sadness. Her story is perhaps not finished, but her commitment to hold all the relationships involved together in tension — without denying the reality of any of her feelings (and, thereby, the concreteness of her own sense of self), is a sign of genuine maturity and growth toward wholeness.

FAILURE IN THE INNER WORLD

We do not *recommend* failure. No one should seek to fail with some notion that the experience will be transforming. When failure strikes, there is a possibility of achieving a perspective which is helpful. But let's not kid ourselves. As Oscar Wilde remarked, "Truth is rarely pure and never simple." The relationship between failure and its rewards is often difficult to trace. And sometimes the "benefits" may be so dwarfed by the cost that the idea of correlating the two may seem absurd.

This is especially true when our sense of failure arises out of some incident or condition of victimization. When others override our power to act and deprive us of our freedom to make constructive, life-enhancing choices, we are left with consequences we had no hand in shaping. This may contribute significantly to a sense of alienation or inauthenticity, and it may be very difficult to know where to begin in setting things right. But with time — and very often with professional help — we can make progress. Even if we never achieve complete healing — with all our pain dispelled — we *can* put our experience back into balance and reclaim to a large extent both our integrity and power.

The following story is a troubling one but still a failure story with hope.

TANYA'S STORY

Although Tanya overcame poverty, put herself through school, raised a son on her own, and has achieved tremendous financial and professional success, she is plagued by an image of herself as a failure. At 29, Tanya is a sophisticated, engaging woman who looks far more mature than her years.

"My mother got divorced from my father before I was born. She was a very naive, young farm girl from Colorado. He had been traveling through town and he took up with her and they got married. For a honeymoon, they traveled to his old home town in Florida. While they were there, the FBI picked him up — I think it was for embezzlement. So she moved back home and found out she was pregnant with me.

"She married again when I was three, and they had two more kids. When I was nine, my stepfather died at 42 of a heart attack. One year before, my mom, who was 27, had been diagnosed as schizophrenic. So we moved back to my mom's hometown, where my grandmother lived in a trailer court. Because my mom was sick, my grandmother was more of a mother figure, but even though she was the most loving person on earth, I don't feel she could accept me. I didn't fit the mold. For a while after my mom became sick I went to live with an aunt and uncle. He was the only man in my life and he was a perfectionist. He didn't like me and thought I was a liar. When I brought home my first report card and it was all Cs he threw it on the floor and said, 'You'll never go to college.'

"I never had anybody tell me I was good at anything. I was never allowed to succeed at anything — I missed 35 days of school in seventh grade and my family wasn't even aware. I remember starting a group when I was in junior high; we worked to collect money to send to Africa. No one ever said, 'Wow, that's good.' I was only criticized for being the way I was. I felt they wanted to carve off all my edges. All the time I was growing up, I never had an identity, except that I was not OK, and a failure.

"My mom was really dissatisfied with her own life and she pushed me to be what she wasn't and wanted to be. When I got older, she told me about how she taught me to tie my shoes, making me retie them and retie them until I got them PERFECT. That's how I was supposed to be.

"When I got pregnant, I really let her down. I was 15 years old and had just broken up with my boyfriend and I found out I was pregnant. It was so unjust — this was from the first intercourse in my life! I decided I was going to prove to my mom that I wasn't going to be the typical pregnant teen, and I wasn't. I already knew how to run a household, because I had been doing that at home. The father and I got back together and I was planning to have the baby and give it up for adoption by a relative. We figured that if we got along well we could get married. So somehow I ended up in this trailer in Nevada, 15 years old, waiting out the end of my pregnancy, having no idea what to expect and no family around for support. I had planned to give the baby to one of my aunts, who couldn't have kids. I remember telling my grandmother about my idea and I didn't get much response from her one way or another. The same day, I was given a baby blanket. Between the lack of expressed support for my plan from my family and the sentimentality the baby blanket brought up in me, I decided on the spot to keep the baby. It was due that day.

"I had a little boy. My husband quit his job, and I let him know that if we were going to be a family, we had to eat — and I went back home to my mom. I finished up grades 10 and 11 in a year, took another year to graduate, then started selling insurance door-to-door in order to finance college. I was selling with other girls. One of them knew a potential client — he was with a group of semiprofessional boxers who were on the circuit. This girl and I went out to a house in the suburbs, apparently to meet with the client. It turned into a big party. I wasn't a drinker, and I don't remember having much, but after a while I lay down on a pile of coats to sleep. I felt drugged — I still wonder whether I was. Four guys came in one at a time and raped me. I couldn't move — couldn't fight back. I tried to talk them out of it. I said, 'I'm only 16, I have a kid at home, leave me alone,' but they didn't stop.

"When they were gone I found my coat and climbed out the window. I felt so ashamed — I thought I had done something wrong! I didn't want to disturb the girl who had brought me, so I went roaming through the streets in the middle of the night, not wanting to disturb anybody, looking for a house with lights on. I found one and called a taxi, and had him take me to an all-night restaurant where I waited until I felt it was a decent hour to call my boss. I didn't want to disturb him, either! At 7:30 I called him and said, 'Come get me, something bad has happened.' After I told him he said I shouldn't make a big deal out of it because it would be bad — if my husband found out he might make me quit my job. That seemed to make sense to me so I didn't press it. I went home and told my husband I wanted a divorce.

"It doesn't get better quite yet. I did manage to put myself through college, although the last two years were the most depressing, isolated and powerless years of my life. I lived through this — the poverty, the isolation, and the pain of taking care of my child — mostly just with an overwhelming sense of insecurity about everything. After I graduated from college and got my first professional job, I went through what I now think was a delayed reaction to the rape: a severe depression.

"Because of these experiences, and the fact that I seemingly survived them so well, most people think I'm very successful, but I'm plagued by a deep, unfaltering sense of failure. I've been through a lot of therapy and it's helped a great deal with self-esteem issues. I have no apparent reason to feel like a failure — but yet it persists no matter how objective I am. I do demand perfection of myself, which I probably got from my childhood. So I'm constantly on myself for not exercising enough, not being thin enough, organized enough, not having a big enough vocabulary.

"Slowly, I'm able to claim my abilities and get some sense of my own identity. At first, all I knew about myself was that I was a responsible parent. Now, I have a few more words — resourceful, attractive, persistent. It's so weird not to have an identity for yourself, but it takes time to see it. I have a big need for control, which I think is partly a consequence of the rape, and partly a childhood in which I had so little say. It makes it hard to develop a relationship, because there's this big wall up there when I meet someone.

"One success I have been able to acknowledge is my son. Last summer he was very sick with an illness that took a lot of time and trouble to diagnose. At first they thought it was psychological, but ultimately they found a medical cause. But in the process of getting a diagnosis, I was meeting and talking with so many people — doctors, nurses, social workers, the works. And I got so many compliments on what a great kid he is. They said, 'you have so much to be proud of — you've obviously been a good parent.' And these are people who deal with kids all the time! So I listened, and I'm starting to take some of the credit for the fact that he is such a hot ticket.

"In terms of society's definition of success, I'm in great shape. My career has gone from strength to strength. I have been involved in high-tech sales for the last several years, and consistently fall in the top 10% — and several times I've been number one. I just landed the job I've been working toward my whole career — it's the kind of position where you'll find cream-of-the-crop sales professionals. It's very competitive, very challenging. I expect to make well over $100,000 after my second year. Of course, landing this job was very stressful — I always assume I won't be able to do something, even when I've proven over and over that I can. So I just go back to my counselor, and she helps me remind myself of what I have already accomplished.

"No one in my family knows how to deal with me. When I graduated from college, they didn't know what to say. Here I am in a great job, and I think they're absolutely floored. My plan is to make piles of money, save a chunk of it, and maybe go into business for myself. I'd also like to get involved in volunteer work, especially with pregnant teens. But my biggest challenge is to keep working on just feeling comfortable with me."

Tanya has come a long way from the traumas and mistakes of her youth and has found much success in her adult life, yet she carries with her the wounds of those earlier mishaps. Despite much evidence on the *outside* to the contrary, she feels like a failure in certain sensitive areas of her *inner* being. We can probably assume that a judgment ("I am a failure") has been made by this person, however long ago or unconsciously. That judgment is both dubious and unnecessary: dubious because it expresses an opinion voiced by one whose ability to judge has been severely compromised; unnecessary because "failure" implies a finality which does not adequately take into account the fact that "life goes on."

When we ask the question "Why does this person feel like a failure?" we discover once again a link between failure and inauthenticity: the one who makes the judgment "I am a failure" is wounded, "not-all-there," not fully herself, less than herself, other than herself, invaded, violated, robbed, diminished, forced by trauma to live out of touch with an important part of her soul or psyche. In this case, largely due to a specific event (the rape) she has found herself to be living an inauthentic existence. Inauthenticity (incompleteness, lack of wholeness) in "the textbook case" eventually collapses — bringing on the failure crisis and healing. This has not happened and perhaps cannot happen. The wound is too deep. It may be that the innermost self, the self that is both the driving force and the "blueprint" for the ideal wholeness, is itself damaged. The ideal has been desecrated. The blueprint is illegible. If healing originates from within and if the innermost self is traumatized, then healing is a long, slow and difficult process. A Jungian or a transpersonal psychologist or a religious person might assert that there exists outside of the self other resources for healing. It may also be that over time, with enough evidence of her success supplied to her consistently by people whom she trusts, Tanya will have so much information that contradicts her own negative self-assessment that she will be able to revise the way she sees herself.

Tanya came to bat with almost three strikes against her, among them severe difficulties with family and money. Even without the rape experience, she would have had much to overcome. Contemporary rape counseling workers report that the damage done by such violation not just of the body but also the mind can take years to repair. Given the distance she has traveled, Tanya's story may be the greatest success story in this book.

FAILURE CROSSING THE BOUNDARIES OF INNER AND OUTER LIFE

The final story in this chapter is an example of how failure occurs in different areas of life all at once. Failure is not a localized phenomena. At times of crisis, when our attention is so forcibly directed at one particular situation (which we identify as the "failure"), this interconnectedness may become obscure. Nevertheless, the notion that different areas of experience — work, love, health — are *unrelated* is an abstraction that we make for reasons of our own. Likewise, the idea that we are individuals who can live outside of relationship to others and to our environment is a fiction which sometimes may be helpful and sometimes may not. The following story is an example of how failure arising in several areas of life, brought about both seemingly insuperable difficulties and important opportunities for reevaluation and self-understanding.

ELIOT'S STORY

In his early 40s, Eliot is fun to be with and fascinating to listen to. His love of language and learning is obvious in his articulate conversation, and his sense of balance about life is reflected in the combination of seriousness and mirth that he brings to the telling of his story. Lack of balance in his life is the primary cause he points to in the simultaneous loss of his job and end of his marriage — and the result of these experiences the beginning of a new approach to life.

> "I grew up in a very dark home. Although I know my parents felt a lot of love for me and my younger brother, they were dealing with so many problems that home life was pretty joyless. My parents were pillars of the church and community, and in fact they contributed greatly to the outside world — my father was a successful businessman in town and chairman

of the congregation at the church, my mother was director of the youth group. Dad was active in Rotary... from the outside it looked like the perfect family. Inside, though, we were in the grips of massive, insistent, rigorously disciplined denial. Part of the denial was around my father's alcoholism, but there were other things too — a paranoid, hypochondriacal grandmother who lived with us, her abuse of my father, all sorts of problems that were never acknowledged, let alone addressed. I lived in a family who failed to take good care of themselves, although they tried to take care of each other, and who failed to lift that suffocating cloud of denial.

"So I looked outside the home for happiness and success in life. I was a high achiever in school — I fought hard to get to be president of my class, get onto varsity or onto the yearbook — I think I chose those things because they all involved passionate commitments to activities that allowed for joyful outcomes, and my home life was pretty joyless. I took the energy my parents put into socially responsible activity and routed it into athletics, creativity — I wanted the rush, the victory, the celebration. My brother, who was seven years younger, did the same thing in his own way. He was the 'party boy,' and the caption written under his photo in his high school yearbook was 'every night is Saturday night!' It was made for him.

"When I was in eighth grade I was 'Wonderboy,' — president of the class, on all the teams, piling on the badges in Boy Scouts (it's nauseating to me when I look back on it!). I was in a public school, but in the neighborhood there was a wonderful private day school, and their coaches were always on the lookout for good prospective students for the high school. Two of us were invited to take an entrance exam for scholarships — we did, and we were offered scholarships and then enrolled. This was a big decision for me, to leave the public school track and go off in this direction. Socially, it was another planet. I went to this private school for a year and I just hated it. At the end of the year, after a lot of begging and pleading on my part, my parents let me go back to the public school. They weren't harsh with me, but I'm sure they were disappointed. I think they thought this was a failure on my part — they were living out their own fantasies about climbing the social ladder through me. As it turned out, by the time I finished high school, I was Wonderboy all over again, so I guess I had redeemed myself.

"Perhaps returning to the public school was a healthy decision on my part, but it is symptomatic of something of a trend. Turning my back on opportunity has happened at several very significant junctures, and it is typical of what I see as the most puzzling sorts of failures in my life. This is the scenario: Opportunity knocks, I do not answer the door. Or if I do answer the door, I say, 'So, what exactly is it you're selling?' And we get into this long dialogue that sometimes lasts a couple of years while I'm hemming and hawing about 'is it a good deal or not a good deal? Maybe I should wait for another deal? A better deal?' And pretty soon Opportunity is sitting across the table from me drumming its fingers, and the awful thing is I don't hear this tapping on the table. I don't realize I'm running out of time. And inevitably Opportunity mumbles, 'I'm sorry, I have another appointment . . .' and shuffles back out the door.

"An example of this is that I was invited to apply to Harvard, and I didn't. When it was time to think about graduate school, I didn't try for the best universities, even though I was a strong student. I wonder whether this had to do with doubting whether I could do the very best or whether, in fact, I felt I deserved the very best. The most devastating example of this was a love affair I had. She was, you could say, the 'Harvard of my romantic life.' She came along after the breakup of my marriage, and we spent four years together. She was someone who represented the kind of energy and life I wanted to associate myself with — I still considered myself a staid, overly rational intellectual; she was an exciting, dynamic, lusty artist. After two wonderful years together, she was 'knocking on my door' proposing marriage. I wasn't able to seize the opportunity. My feelings told me this was a good relationship, but my mind got in the way. I kept looking for some kind of intellectual or rational confirmation — kicking the tires, so to speak — not realizing that *information* by itself is never going to help you make this kind of decision. I hedged my bets, I hesitated. And eventually the relationship ended. I spent a lot of time in the years following that, regretting my inability to reach out and seize something that my heart wanted, even if my mind couldn't confirm the decision. I see this as an example of a failure to 'follow my bliss,' to borrow Joseph Campbell's phrase.

"About ten years ago, and before the relationship I've been talking about, I had what you might call a multisystem failure. I had traveled comfortably and obviously from college to graduate school and inevitably to the life of academe. Becoming a professor was a direct, linear extension of being a good student. I became a history professor at a small liberal arts college. After seven years, two others and I were eligible for tenure. Of course I had a lot invested in getting tenure — it is the academic's seal of approval and source of career security. I sat on the faculty evaluation committee that year, and was asked to vote against tenure for those other two people whose records were in fact just fine. I abstained — I wasn't courageous enough to go to the dean and refuse to play along with some plan he had. So I knew the situation was ugly, but that still didn't prepare me for being denied tenure myself. If I had been lighter of foot I might have been able to look at that situation and say, 'God forgive you if this is what you guys want to do with your lives, but as for me, there's a big world out there and here I go.' Instead, I chose to fight. I chose to struggle to justify myself in their eyes, to prove to them that they were wrong. And you know, I got almost all the way through it. I got the whole faculty to review the committee's decision and they reversed their decision, and wrote a two-inch-thick report. But that still didn't do any good, because the administrators on the top had decided they wanted to get rid of three people, and they got rid of them.

"I took it so seriously! I thought I had no alternatives. I thought that if I couldn't prevail in the case then I was weak. Now, when I look back, part of what I see is that I wasn't willing to let go soon enough. And I don't mean to suggest that one should not hold the steering wheel firmly and stay on the course, but if you're really listening to your heart and paying attention to what's going on around you, you have a better chance of being able to recognize when the moment has come when you can't win. The point is, there are so many other situations out there waiting for you to succeed at — or even fail at — you might as well go.

"This loss marked the end of that career. At the same time as my tenure was being denied, my marriage was failing. At about the same time, my father died, my cat died, my best friend moved away, and the love affair I had that was part of the demise of the marriage crashed and burned. So in the space of eight months I had four or five of most of the loss experiences that most people spread out over maybe 20 years. I don't think it is a coincidence that my career and marriage were failing at the same time. I think that what was dying there — and I read it then as failure on my part but I see it now as something that was dying in an organic, natural sense — was that my life was out of balance. I've been working on this ever since, and I think I'll probably go on struggling with it forever, but I think in this past ten years of my life, I've seen it for what it is. I think this problem is rooted in the family — that is where I learned how to be a success in those areas where the family couldn't get at me, which is outside the home, in intellectual or creative activity, in sports. In the areas where emotions were involved, and open, honest, face-to-face communication, and the expression of love and anger and all those feelings, my parents were walking around in a fog. So even though they modeled for me very effectively how to go out in the world and perform well, they could not model how to perform well at home. They showed me how to do well, but they couldn't show me how to be well. And of course I was stuck with those limitations when I chose my career, and they led to my broken marriage. It took years, and a lot of work and a lot of time and tears and shouting and hundreds of pages of psychological drivel written into my journal. The tears and shouting and endless writing about myself were a lot like lancing a boil — you must cut it and get the stuff out. Then you can begin to heal, to renew.

"What 'cuts it' is a spiritual energy, I think. It's whatever it is that puts the fire in our souls — that's what cuts it. It is not rational. It has nothing to do with intelligence. It must have something to do with grace. I think there are some things you can do to make yourself a little more open to grace. One of them is to be quiet, to get unbusy in your head if you can. But I don't think there's much else you can do, and the fact that lots of people go through their lives and never seem to hear it or see it at all is a mystery I can't explain. I think about my brother — he died recently after a ten-year-long suicide by alcohol. I wonder about him — why didn't a voice full of grace speak to my brother?

"I think, having had these experiences in my life, I have at long last become somewhat lighter of foot. I have a stronger and better sense of my ability to make a living, and I've been able to redirect my energies and fashion a fulfilling career. I am comfortable with the fact that almost every rich and interesting life I've ever heard about has had some colossal failures; so mine don't seem so lonely alongside them. I've gotten better at listening to my heart and following what I hear. I am happy in a new relationship. Things are going along pretty well at this point in my life, and I'm pleased to be who I am."

THIRD EXERCISE

This is a time for creative rediscovery. Through the following three questions, you will have a chance to reaffirm your gifts, your achievements and your personal values. Because the failure experience seems so often to be linked with losing touch with our true selves, we all need to find ways of being reintroduced. Let this be a first step for you. Allow yourself to enjoy this exercise — set aside at least an hour for it if you can. Then give your imagination free rein!

A. List 15 (or more) times in your life when you felt most completely yourself. These are times when you felt most peaceful, centered, connected with a higher power, happiest, or most satisfied. These may be times spent alone or with someone, and they may have significance only for you. Once you have done this, choose the five that hold the most meaning for you. Mark them.

B. List 15 (or more) experiences in your life when you felt you really used your gifts well. Examples will include verbs such as creating, building, caring, organizing, problem solving, enjoying, etc. These could be drawn from any time in your life, from childhood until today. Consider experiences in school, at work, in your community, in relationships. There may be some overlapping with part A of this exercise. Once you have listed them, select the five you feel most strongly about. Mark them.

C. Look at the responses you wrote down in part A, paying special attention to the five you highlighted. What personal gifts or talents were you using then? Your response might include such things as "ability to listen" or "playfulness." Write them down.

D. Look over the responses you made to the three questions above. Meditate on them for a few minutes. Allow your mind to bring them together. Consider what each has directed your attention to and how each fits in with the whole. Is it hard for you to focus on positive elements in your story? If so, why? Once you've spent some time allowing the pattern of your responses to speak to you, write down what you see emerging from your reflection. Do you see any interconnectedness between, on the one hand, these lists of times of satisfaction and pleasing performance and, on the other, lists of times when you were at odds with yourself or when you failed?

E. Think of five people whom you admire. They may be known to you personally living or dead, real or fictitious. (Don't be surprised if your list turns out to be something like, "Abraham Lincoln, Mickey Mouse, Mom, Gandhi and Sally Ride.") One at a time, each will speak to you. Close your eyes and imagine that this person is sitting right in front of you, with a message for you. Imagine that this person knows you very well and wants to tell you about the special qualities, gifts, or abilities that you have. In fact, this person *admires* you! Once you have pictured this person in your mind's eye, listen to what he or she has to say to you. Don't be embarrassed; allow each to speak to you with enthusiasm, admiration and love. Write down these positive comments and repeat the process with each of the five people.

(This exercise was adapted from the work of Barbara Sher, in her book *Wishcraft: How to Get What You Really Want.*)

F. Look over what you've written in Part E. What qualities or personal values are represented here? Which do you care about most? Think back to the failure experience you chose to work with in previous exercises, and explore whether the values you identified here were involved in that experience.

How does the person you've been writing about in this exercise compare to the person you were in your failure experience? What does this say to you?

FAILURE AS THREEFOLD PROCESS
Crisis, Stuckness, Breaking Free

Next week there can't be any crisis. My schedule is already full.
HENRY KISSINGER

THERE IS A THREEFOLD PATTERN to many of the descriptions of crisis reported by our interviewees. First, there was the initial experience of failure. We have discussed several aspects of this stage in the previous chapter.

Second, there was a stage characterized by an adaptation to failure, where one lives in a constant state of defensiveness. Initially, this withdrawal from life may be necessary, providing the individual with a badly needed opportunity to recover from the initial shock brought on by failure. Eventually, however, this diminishment of life's normal activity becomes habitual, and instead of providing a place of refuge, the individual may feel imprisoned or stuck.

The third stage comes about at the point of collapse of this constrained and limited existence. Here, crisis — as a way of life — itself goes into crisis. The *élan vital*, the urge

145

toward growth and wholeness, overcomes the sense of imprisonment and the individual begins to reclaim both freedom and personal power.

This chapter takes a step back to gain perspective on each of these phases of the overall failure experience: *Crisis, Stuckness,* and *Breaking Free.*

Bear in mind, however, as we do, that all such talk about "stages" or "phases" in the process of human development are abstractions, conceived to help us get a handle on experience (including thoughts and feelings) that is always, at best, elusive and hard to pin down definitively. You will note in this chapter's discussion of a threefold process of failure-as-useful-crisis the conspicuous absence of comments about *timetables.* There aren't any timetables for dealing with failure; you have to make your own. And what one person passes through quickly, in a few months, another person may need a few years to absorb and comprehend. Each of us marches to the beat of a different drummer. The point is that it's *your* drum, and you must pay attention to the beat.

CRISIS

What is required is that we should break free of certain habits of thinking and perceiving that have become natural for us. We must return to the direct perception of change and mobility. Movement is reality itself! Before this spectacle of universal mobility there may be some who will be seized with dizziness. They are accustomed to terra firma; they cannot get used to the rolling and pitching. They must have "fixed" points to which they can attach thought and existence. They think that if everything passes, nothing exists! The material world, they say, is going to disintegrate, and the mind will drown in the torrent-like flow of things.

— Let them be reassured! Change, if they consent to look directly at it without an interposed veil, will very quickly appear to them to be the most substantial and durable thing possible.

HENRI BERGSON
[from *The Creative Mind*]

Erika Schuchardt, professor at Hanover University in Germany, has identified eight distinct stages in the process of coming to terms with failure. Her essay, entitled "Coping With Failure 'Why Me?' Opportunities for Learning to Live," describes a spiraling pattern of thoughts and feelings that goes through an initial phase where Uncertainty about what exactly has occurred eventually gives way to Certainty. Within this spiral there are three intermediate stages — reminiscent of Kubler-Ross's Death & Dying scheme — Negotiation, Depression, and Acceptance.

Schuchardt: *Acceptance does not so much mean resigned surrender as a state of contentment. Acceptance is not assent and affirmation. No one can readily affirm severe losses, but individuals can learn to accept the inevitable in coping with their crises. So there is acceptance in crossing the limits of one's consciousness, which now expectedly widen. That makes acceptance possible.*[1]

The final two stages include Activity, a "regrouping" and a "restructuring," during which an active engagement with life resumes and increases. Solidarity, the final stage — not attained by everyone — where the experience of the individual's crisis, "now seen in relation to a wider sphere of life," is characterized by a commitment to take the lessons learned through failure out into society.

Crisis is change. In each instance when we encounter some great emotional shock — the pain of separation, or loss, or disappointment, or any similar experience of anguish — we may feel that describing what is happening to us merely as "change" is inadequate. The word seems hardly capable of conveying the nature of what has befallen us. From an emotional standpoint, this may very well be true. But if we take the dynamic perspective — which eventually we must do if we are to move through crisis and on into new life — then change has to be seen as the very heart of the process of growth.

When we consider how change operates in other aspects of life, the picture may become a little clearer. A child growing up experiences change almost continuously. Bodily growth, new skills, more responsibilities, expanding knowledge. Adults and children can see change happening all around them without any great need for introspection. The cycle of the seasons, the rising and falling of the tide, the growth of ice crystals on a window pane, the ripening of a tomato. These and dozens of other examples that anyone can recall without difficulty demonstrate that change is universal. Change does not interrupt the flow of life. *Change is the flow of life.* It is only when change sweeps away relationships or circumstances that have been dear or important to us that change is then seen as crisis.

In the process of transforming failure into a reward worth keeping, crisis is not necessarily to be avoided. To put it another way, necessary crisis is not to be avoided. Crisis, or at least change, is an indispensable aspect of growth. To deny or evade the experience of needed change — painful though it may be — is to turn away from life.

The concept of crisis has a long and distinguished pedigree. I remember in high school — a time full of crises of all shapes and sizes — the lectures in English class on the role crisis plays in literature. For the Greek tragic characters, their pride, which is usually a distinguishing heroic attribute, exceeds its natural limits. They become arrogant; literally, they arrogate to themselves a power and authority which surpasses that which is appropriate to their mortal status. They seek to become like gods. This leads to *hubris*, an act of overweening pride upon which their destiny turns. They are brought low. One gets murdered in the bath. Another brings down destruction on his city or civilization. Their children get killed. Or they kill their children. Or their children kill them and so on. They fail, big time. These experiences following the act of *hubris* are crises. But the progress of character development as given in this literary model — nearly two and a half thousand years ago — does not end here. Crisis leads to catharsis or change.

Another characteristic of a failure crisis is that it is a *boundary* experience. In other words, crisis brings an individual to the edge of his or her world and up to that frontier where one is faced with one's own limitations and possibilities. The view from this vantage point can be unfamiliar and terrifying. In his book *Crisis Experience in Modern Life*, Charles Gerkin, professor of pastoral psychology at Emory University, describes the boundary experience as follows:

> *A crisis situation is, for modern persons, an extreme or boundary situation in which the fundamental contradiction between human aspirations and finite possibilities becomes visible in such a way as to demand attention. In that situation a most elemental choice is forced upon persons. Either [they] must defend themselves against the contradiction with whatever human defense is possible, be that denial or heroic courage, or they must open themselves to the vulnerability of the unknown future.*[2]

To become open to uncertainty in one's own life is no easy matter. We have a host of cliches from which to choose to describe, in simple terms, what is actually a delicate, subtle, difficult matter. "Let it be." "Go with the flow." "Don't worry — be happy." And so on. All such cliches may contain kernels of truth, but the truth is not a simple one. Should the individual choose not to open himself to uncertainty, it will be easy to evade the failure crisis indefinitely. There are many available distractions. Throwing oneself headlong into work or play one can find refuge from the confrontation with the problem of the present moment. In the words of philosopher Martin Buber, "Life becomes a series of hideouts."

Denial of a failure crisis, through addictive behavior — such as drinking alcohol, using drugs, overworking — or *distraction* through some form of entertainment — television, movies, sporting events, and the like — are typical strategies individuals use to keep themselves from looking at the real circumstances of their lives. Even psychotherapy can offer such an escape should an individual in unwitting collusion with the therapist become involved in an unnaturally long process that amounts to an escape from reality. In such an instance, the original objective of healing becomes subordinated to the relationship between the client and the therapist, which in turn becomes an end in itself, thereby producing "therapeutic process addiction" and "therapy junkies" (and, presumably "therapy pushers").

The real and present danger for a person in failure is that the crisis can become stabilized without being addressed. The great peril here is that — should the failure crisis be accepted and not dealt with — a pervasive dull sense of malaise is sure to infect the whole of the individual's life. His or her life and failure crisis are thus yoked together in an uneasy bondage, stuck, as it were, between what is past and could be done with, and what waits to be.

My dictionary gives the first definition of "catharsis" as "purgation, especially of the bowels." (Interesting metaphor, the application of which I leave up to the reader!). Originally, it referred to the cleansing of the character in the drama by a punishment which was administered directly or indirectly by the gods in and through the character's crisis. Speaking more broadly, this was a clearing of the character's existential condition, the fix or dilemma he's in, and a recovery of the proper balance of relationships in the cosmos. Psychiatrically speaking, catharsis is defined as that process which relieves fears, anxieties, and so forth, by bringing them into consciousness where they may be considered in the therapeutic milieu.

All these definitions of catharsis (including the one having to do with clearing the bowels) have significance for our discussion of failure. This book proposes that we add an emphasis to the *dynamic* qualities of crisis that lead, when catharsis is achieved, to a new sense of the self — one that is more than merely a restoration of what came before. He, or she, who fails, and profits from it, is never the same again.

STUCKNESS

We are the hollow men

We are the stuffed men

Leaning together

Headpiece filled with straw. Alas!

Our dried voices, when

We whisper together

Are quiet and meaningless
As wind in dry grass
Or rats' feet over broken glass
In our dry cellar

Shape without form, shade without color,
Paralyzed force, gesture without motion;

Those who have crossed
With direct eyes, to death's other Kingdom
Remember us — if at all — not as lost
Violent souls, but only
As the hollow men
The stuffed men.

T. S. ELIOT

One of the great dangers in a failure crisis experience is that it may become arrested, prevented from moving into new life beyond. These lines excerpted from T. S. Eliot's "The Hollow Men" describe in a chillingly evocative way the deadliness of a life where even crisis becomes a dull and interminable condition. Of all the stories we collected, those which described the bleakness of a life of "quiet desperation," to borrow Henry David Thoreau's phrase, were the most disturbing. That these individuals could have fallen beyond the reach of refreshing, rejuvenating relationships, and could have been brought instead to a state where their experiences only confirm and reinforce their sense of defeat is tragic and even pathetic. The following story typifies the condition of one who has become "stuck" in failure. Like one of "the hollow men," there is about the writer a deep sense of loss, emptiness and futility. Even a lifetime of crisis has been unable to dislodge the sense of failure deeply embedded in his spirit.

JOE'S STORY

"So you want to hear about failure? I'll give you failure. I'm a 52-year-old white male whose life has been a series of disasters. I don't know if my failures have contributed to a richer life, but I'll tell you about me anyway.

"My first significant setback (not really a failure) was when my mother died when I was 10 years old. It was a great loss for me — people who knew me say that I've never recovered from that loss.

"I remember getting a few bad grades in high school, but no Fs. I did well enough in high school to get into a good college. There I received my first F, in a sociology class, of all things. My dad (he never re-married) wanted me to be a physician. (I didn't know what I wanted to do with my life — I considered dropping out of college and entering the Navy, but I was underage and my father wouldn't sign the necessary papers). I started college as a pre-med, but low grades in elementary chemistry convinced me that I wasn't going to make it to med school. I then became a French major, but soon started getting low grades and decided to work toward going to law school. My grades continued to be quite low, and I was put on academic probation. I managed to graduate in 1968 with a low C average. I applied to and was accepted at a decent law school. I spent an unhappy year there (I wasn't sure I wanted to be a lawyer, or anything else). Sure enough, I flunked out at the end of the year.

"I returned home and got my first real job — driving a cab. I actually enjoyed the work and did it off and on over the next 15 years. I then decided to become a school teacher, after being reminded many times that I was wasting my time and educational background merely by driving a taxi. I found the academic training to be much easier than undergraduate or law school, and managed to get my teaching credentials. I taught high school and junior high school social studies, mostly in the inner-city schools. I never really liked teaching and never felt I was very effective at it. Principals would disapprove of my performance and transfer me to another school — three or four times in my fourteen years. The school district finally got tired of me, and I was dismissed eight years ago. By that time, I was ready to quit, but I let them fire me.

"I might insert at this point that I am married — the same woman for 12 years. My wife has been employed by the same company for almost 20 years. We have a 10-year-old daughter, who is an honor roll student in school and does well in all aspects of life. It is not a perfect marriage, but it has lasted, in spite of numerous setbacks.

"I took another 'menial' job, this time as a courier in an entertainment industry-related company. I was 45 years old at the time. I applied for a few jobs in the insurance field, but was rejected. I no longer wanted to teach or go back to school to learn a new career. After about a year of driving around town, delivering items for the music industry (again, I enjoyed the work, even though I was making only a little over minimum wage, tearing up a good car used for deliveries, and we were having trouble making ends meet

— mortgage payments, two car payments, insurance, private school tuition for my daughter, and so on) — I decided to open my own business.

"Another failure! I used my teacher retirement funds and other savings to buy a convenience store in a high-rise building. It looked pretty good at the start, but business quickly fell off. I figure I lost about $60,000 cash, my first real financial failure. I went back to work for the delivery service, knowing it would be difficult to make ends meet, although somehow my wife and I manage to. In the last three or four years I have also done some school teaching, as a substitute. I have been dismissed by about four different school districts, each time for poor performance. I made quite a bit of money by selling our home in the city in 1988. We moved to a small town about 100 miles away and bought a less expensive home. I also inherited some money when my father died a year ago.

"I am presently unemployed, and have spent almost all the money I just mentioned. My wife is still working. I spend my days watching TV, reading, taking long walks and bike rides, and paddling my kayak around a nearby lake.

"About a week ago, I took a test for city planner — I failed the test. It was very technical, I wasn't prepared for it."

What are we to make of such a story? It is tempting to psychologize. Joe's immediate mention of his mother's death when he was still a young child could easily lead us to draw inferences between this early loss and all his subsequent failures. The one example he does give of a job at which he succeeded and that he enjoyed was driving a taxi. What was it that prevented him from recognizing that this might have been a starting place for him? Instead of leaving this activity to find "a real job," why could he not have continued doing what he liked to see where it might lead him? Given the limited information we received (a letter), it seems unwise to speculate what the answers to these questions might be. Rather, let this story stand as an example of what can become of one who — for whatever reason — becomes a victim of his own existence. To live beyond the reach even of crisis means that the recurring experiences of failure, which should have shaken him to the very core, could not produce their cathartic effect. The result is a deadening of the spirit and a diminishing of constructive and active engagement with the world. Fortunately, in many cases (and we can only hope that Joe's will be one, too), the attenuated crisis and pattern of habitual failure will not indefinitely resist the demand for new growth that life makes on us. Most of us cannot perpetually escape the call to get back into the business of living! Indeed, Joe's story illustrates "stuckness" in the extreme. Although he indicates what he likes and dislikes, he does not tell us whether he knows *why* some jobs and activities are good for him while others are not. And not knowing *why*, it appears that he is trapped in a cycle of failure repetitions. Like Sisyphus, he pushes the rock up the hill only to find that it always comes down again. As George Santayana said, "Those who cannot remember the past are condemned to repeat it." Joe appears to be stuck because he has not yet "remembered" his own personal "past" deeply enough to glean the insights which could empower him to transcend it.

Most people's failure crises include a period of stuckness, although much more brief than Joe's. Nevertheless, the same kinds of feelings of dull, inevitable repetition can characterize a short period of stuckness as well as a life-long one. This phase of the failure crisis carries the individual across dangerous waters.

BREAKING FREE

Ironically, when the call to move forward and out of the failure crisis finally gets through, it too may appear as heralding another crisis: anything that brings about a change from what is known and familiar — even stuckness and defeat — produces anxiety. In my own case, coming to the point where I could get past seeing myself as a failure was a lengthy process that involved moving to a new town, ending certain relationships with people who would not or could not see that I had changed, and searching out new relationships that would hold me accountable to my claims of new life and growth.

Another important development in my own failure story, which only began to occur at this latter stage of my progress through crisis, was the radical reappraisal of everything that had happened to me in my failure experience. It began with little revelations, intimations that the goal I had been seeking for so long was already achieved, almost unbeknownst to me, and that all the misadventures that had helped to bring the failure crisis to pass were not, from my new perspective, failures at all but, to borrow Judith Viorst's useful phrase, "necessary losses" in my struggle to grow.[3]

The dawning of such insights about one's movement through the later stage of a failure crisis can come about in the most unexpected times and places. One respondent described to us how the breakthrough in his understanding came about as he was walking across a ballfield.

"We had so little money. We never had any money, really! Not for years, it seems. And what we had wasn't really ours. It belonged to our extended family of creditors. Both my wife and I had serious business and professional failures that occurred one right on top of the other. It put us back to the same financial state we were in when we first got out of school.

"Well, one week — this was in the early spring — we did manage to raise a little cash from the many projects we had going on all the time. We put it in the bank and felt that we had bought a month or so of breathing room. Then the car died. And, of course, it didn't just die. It died, was fixed, died again, was fixed again. It was some problem with the electrical system and it took them three weeks and three different mechanics to figure it out. Not having the car was a problem. We had kids to take to school. Classes and meetings to attend ourselves, and things like laundry and groceries had to be carried back the half-mile or so to the apartment. And we could only guess at how much all this was going to cost us.

"One morning during school vacation I was walking my son to the YMCA, where we had signed him up for a week-long mini-camp. This was the third day and the novelty of the walk had worn off. It was muddy and cold and the neighborhood was drab and uninteresting. I remember feeling quite pissed off at the whole state of affairs. Well, on my way home I was crossing the athletic field next to our apartment building. As I got out to the middle, the sun broke through the clouds and for a few minutes there was some relief from all the grayness and dreariness. It was like a switch had been turned on. And something in me came a little bit back to life."

His letter goes on to describe what occurred to him during that moment: the realization that he had already achieved everything that had ever been of any real worth to him: his marriage was happy and sound and he and his wife were committed to each other, he had two beautiful children who were thriving and happy, he was living in a part of the country where he could pursue all of his interests, professionally he was moving in a direction that suited him perfectly, and for which he was receiving all the right kinds of support and affirmation.

In other words, he found — somewhat to his astonishment — that when thinking about himself, the word "failure" no longer applied. He knew that somehow, through a combination of continued effort and a little grace, the bills would get paid.   From this point, everything began to change, as the journey through his failure crisis ended and a significant personal transformation began.

Is there any practical step-by-step advice to be given here, about breaking free of failure, from a psychological or spiritual viewpoint? Our research indicates that the answer is no. There is no how-to manual for getting through the stages of failure. But we can see that the patterns described thus far in this book are widespread, if not universal. An individual going through a failure almost cannot help being helped if he or she will keep an eye out for the signs indicating which phase or stage is passing by. Making an effort to *understand* the failure *is* required. Opening oneself to *acceptance* of things as they are is required, whether this means facing personal limitations or acknowledging that some one (the boss, your spouse) or some thing (the economy) on the "outside" contributed to your failure. When the deepest understanding and acceptance that you can develop have been realized, then the likelihood of a transformation, small or large, in your life becomes real as well. Failure's reward is then ready to manifest itself.

FOURTH EXERCISE

Your journey began by looking at your inherited beliefs about failure and success, and by recollecting an experience that felt to you like failure. Next, through several exercises, you reminded yourself about who you have been, and about what is important to you. What follows is an opportunity to reach another part of yourself, another source of knowing, through a visualization exercise. The subconscious is always at work and is a tremendous source of information and guidance. This exercise is a way of tapping that resource. Gather together some paper and markers, pens, or crayons. Find a quiet, comfortable spot, and follow these directions. If you have someone you trust who could read them aloud to you, and with whom you can share and explore this experience, so much the better. After you have read the instructions for each step, allow your eyes to close so that you can visualize the scene and focus more clearly on your response. When you feel ready, you can record your response and move on to the next step.

A. First, allow yourself to become comfortable and relaxed, releasing tension and breathing slowly and deeply.

Allow yourself to let go of thoughts and to become quietly aware.

B. Imagine you are walking through a wooded glen. It is a warm afternoon. See the sun shining through the treetops. Feel the path beneath your feet. Smell the scents of the woods. Hear the sounds. Take your time to experience the scene.

You come to a clearing, where you are met by a special guide. This is someone who cares deeply about you and knows you very well. Your guide has something to show you.

Your guide leads you to a pool of water, and you gaze into the pool. Beneath the surface of the water you see a scene from your past — an experience that felt to you like failure. Look closely at the scene, becoming aware of what was happening, who was involved, what you were doing and how you were feeling. Draw or describe this experience below.

C. Your guide leads you away from the water, toward a hill. As you climb you feel lighter, more peaceful. You look forward with expectation to reaching the summit.

Once you arrive at the top, you look out over the landscape. You see a wonderful view. Draw or describe it here.

D. You become aware that your guide has brought you here for a purpose. There is a gift that you are meant to have. It will shed light on the failure experience you just revisited when you gazed into the pool. Your guide offers the gift to you, saying, "This gift will help you integrate your experience and reveal to you its significance."

Draw or describe the gift.

E. You accept the gift, recognizing the truth it holds for you. Your guide leads you back down the hill, past the pool, through the woods to the clearing where you first came together. Say goodbye with thanks, keeping the gift for your journey home. Return to the place where you began.

Describe the significance of this gift.

FAILURE AS RESOURCE
Transformation and Empowerment

If a fir tree had a foot or two like a turtle, or a wing,
Do you think it would just wait for the saw to enter?

You know the sun journeys all night under the earth; if it didn't,
How could it throw up its flood of light in the east?

And salt water climbs with such marvellous swiftness to the sky.
If it didn't, how would the cabbages be fed with the rain?

Have you thought of Joseph lately? Didn't he leave his father in
tears, going?
Didn't he then learn how to understand dreams, and give away
grain?

And that man with the long nose, didn't he leave his country,
forced to,
And only then learned how to travel through the three worlds?

*And you, if you can't leave your country, you could go into
yourself,
And become a ruby mine, open to the gifts of the sun.*

*You could travel from your manhood into the inner man, or
from your womanhood into the inner woman—
By a journey of that sort earth became a place where you find
gold.*

*So leave your complaints and self-pity and internalized death-
energy.
Don't you realize how many fruits have already escaped out of
sourness into sweetness?*

*A good source of sweetness is a teacher, mine is named Shams.
You know that every fruit grows more handsome in the light of
the sun.*

"That Journeys are Good," by RUMI
[version by Robert Bly]

───────────────

*Our capacities to take risks and learn from them depends
heavily on whether we understand action as instrumental or ex-
pressive. The instrumental image, which dominates Western culture, portrays action as a means to predetermined ends, as an
instrument or tool of our intentions. The only possible measure
of such action is whether it achieves the ends at which it is
aimed. Instrumental action is governed by the logic of success
and failure; it discourages us from risk-taking because it values
success over learning, and it abhors failure whether we learn
from it or not.*

Instrumental action always wants to win, but win or lose, it inhibits our learning. If we win, we think we know it all and have nothing more to learn. If we lose, we feel so defeated that learning is a hollow consolation. Instrumental action traps us in a system of praise or blame, credit or shame, a system that gives primacy to goals and external evaluations, devalues the gift of self-knowledge, and diminishes our capacity to take the risks that may yield growth.

I find it fascinating that the most "successful" of all activities — science — is one that rejects success and failure as the primary norms for its acts. For the pure scientist, a failed experiment is no failure at all, but a vital step toward learning the truth. Such "failure" narrows the range of relevant hypotheses to be tested and may contribute some positive findings as well.

PARKER PALMER
[from *The Active Life*]

At 32 I decided really to do my own thinking and see if I could disconnect myself from the games and superstitions and the way society says you had to carry on. I would no longer let somebody say: "You have to earn your living." I said "Forget about all that. Let's see if we really start using our minds, what will we learn? ...The only reason I was able to do what I did, was that circumstances pushed me out of society. I made so many mistakes that I really was an outsider which gave me some perspective.

As a thinker I am absolutely overwhelmed by the fact that nature is trying to do something. She is bringing about evolutionary events that were utterly unpredicted by our forebears. Nobody knew we were going to have radio; nobody knew we were going to have the television; nobody knew we were going to have any of these things; going to fly, or send a rocket to the moon. Evolution is bringing these things in. Therefore, I'm much more impressed with evolution and the universe's designing capability than [I am with] the designing ability of the human being.

So I said, "It seems to me nature is trying to make man a success so he can graduate into an important kind of a function. I see that science is only being applied to killing and destruction. Supposing I apply it to trying to make a man a success. If I could see what could be done that's not being done; if I attended to what nature is trying to do, I might find I got on all right. There would be no authority to hire me, but somebody ought to make the experiment and see if it's not so." And because I was penniless and had no credit, and had a wife and child to support, I made the perfect experimental guinea pig.

I've been through a half century and I find it works. But at no point did I have anything to assure me. It's been absolutely deep end all the time. And my family, and my wife's family, would say during those years "You're absolutely treacherous to do this to your darling dependents." And I would get cold feet and think maybe I am an S.O.B. Then someone would say "Come and take a job over here, you're nice and bright." Whenever I did, everything went all wrong. And whenever I went off the deep end again, everything went all right.

BUCKMINSTER FULLER
[from a taped interview for
the radio show "New Dimensions"]

TRANSFORMATION and EMPOWERMENT

A phenomenon as important and universal as failure invites a wide-ranging and eclectic discussion. Invariably, failures arise out of complicated sets of interactions occurring over an entire lifetime. This moment's failure is grounded in all of your past experience. There are psychological, sociological and spiritual dimensions. When failure occurs, it affects many different areas of life, sometimes all at once: home, work, family, physical health, peace of mind. It is, therefore, both a complex and multilayered phenomenon. This chapter is an attempt to bring together the different strands of our investigation of the failure experience.

As our stories have told us, the experience of failure — wherever and whenever it occurs — is a difficult ordeal. The rewards are there, but the process by which we arrive at them involves a struggle, not only with ourselves, but also with the expectations of parents or peers, the well-intended advice of friends and associates, and the responsibilities we bear to those who depend on us. The din of all these voices can be deafening. In the turmoil we may even lose the sound of our own inner voice. But at some point, perhaps even when we are most distracted and overwhelmed, there is an awareness that the failure has loosened its grip on us. Although the complete reinterpretation of our failure experience may lie months or even years ahead, there is a change, a shift that can be seen even as it just begins to occur.

This is the event that we call transformation, meaning a reconstruction of the way we see things, a changeover to a different form of organization of our experience. This is not a mere rearrangement. We do not simply feel better. We feel differently, about ourselves, about our lives, about everything that touches us.

The reason for this change is not hard to understand. Individuals in the midst of failure may very well experience a deterioration in their self-esteem, and, consequently, may begin to think of themselves as failures (rather than as someone experiencing a specific failure). This negative evaluation is not just a rational judgment. It is packed with emotion. Sorrow, guilt, shame, remorse, anger, resentment, bitterness, apathy, melancholia, and fear are all typical feelings associated with failure. Once our negative assessment of ourselves becomes charged with such powerful feelings, it may exercise an irresistible influence over our lives and our actions, forcing other ideas and information into apparent consistency with it. Everything that happens thereafter seems to confirm the diagnosis "I am a failure."

In an individual's transformation of the failure experience the *idée fixe* of failure is overthrown; it loses its power of definition over what life brings to us. The negative self-judgment is let go; the blaming of others is let go, and thus failure dissolves, revealing — as it loosens its hold — both healing insights about how to work, love, or be in a relationship more constructively, and a new gift of time and energy. Consequently, a more balanced understanding of ourselves — as people capable of both success and failure, not wholly perfect, by any means, but not wholly imperfect either — may begin to assert itself.

Surrender

For many individuals we spoke with, the transformation of failure necessarily involved an element of surrender. Without letting go of that portion of the old self with its negative self-assessment, limiting beliefs, and its too-easy tendency to blame, the process of transformation could not occur. But this is by no means an easy thing to accomplish. It is not rational or subject to control. It tests patience to the maximum. The story that follows illustrates how enormously difficult this surrender, this letting go, can be. In spite of the fact that the individual involved had made tremendous progress in other areas of his life, his capitulation to failure at a decisive point was to throw him back into crisis.

FRED'S STORY

Fred is a dashing-looking gentleman in his late fifties. His red hair shows only a touch of gray and he moves easily and laughs readily. Fred's relaxed and casual appearance and his infectious good spirits are enough to set anyone at ease. It seems hard to believe that at one time his life was devastated by alcoholism, divorce, business failure and a nervous breakdown.

> "When I was growing up success was defined very simply: money. My father was my main influence, and for him having money is what success meant. Not relationships. Not success in school. These things were never stressed that much. We didn't have much and I remember thinking very early on that life always involved a struggle just to survive. I don't ever remember discussing failure but I am pretty sure that it was just the opposite. Failure meant not having money. Also, money was not something everyone could get: an immigrant, my father believed that success was for the chosen few and most of them probably inherited it.
>
> "My father also had a significant failure. When he was a young man he and a partner had the first Ford dealership in town. Well, the partnership failed and he lost that opportunity. From that point on he basically went for security. He took a union job in a machinist shop where — except for a stint as engineer on a ship in the China trade — he remained until he retired. I remember that our dinner table conversa-

tion was full of stories about how the front office didn't understand the workers. He was in constant fear of being laid off. After years of working hard at the same company, the day came for his retirement. They called him into the office and said 'Thanks.' That was it! No money. No watch. Nothing! Just 'thanks.' His fellow workers took up a collection, but those were difficult times and all they came up with was 36 dollars.

"So that was my idea of the working life. You knock yourself out for years and you end up with 36 dollars and a 'Thanks' from the people in the office. That made a big impression on me. I swore I would never work for anyone if I could possibly avoid it. When I was 19 I started my first business making wooden boxes for the vegetable growers and fish packers in the area.

"At 20 I started selling cars and I began to make good money. I married soon after and my first daughter was born eight months later. I moved on from car sales to a variety of retail commission sales jobs: televisions, appliances, things of that sort. Eventually, I ended up in real estate, putting together subdivisions. Things were looking better all the time. Three developments I helped put together sold promptly and I thought I was a real world-beater.

"Then there was an episode that really was a turning point for me. One day while looking around the department stores in our area, I noticed a kitchen product called a Handi-Susan. It was a plastic canister set that attached underneath the cupboard. The product was locally made and had done moderately well, and, for some reason, I decided that this item was a sleeper. I was certain that one day every home in North America would own a Handi-Susan. It would

be as common as a spice rack. I managed to interest a
real estate partner in the idea of bankrolling this venture, and the two of us flew to L.A. to meet with a
plastics manufacturer. I will never forget that day. We
sat in his office — the plant engineer, the president of
the plastics company, my partner and myself. The engineer looked our product over closely and said that
he could knock it off without any trouble. Then the
president picked it up and looking it over carefully,
told us: 'You know, I could make this product. But if
I did, at the price you want to charge, it will never
sell.' We were indignant. What was the matter with
this guy? Couldn't he see what a gold mine we had
here? No, he couldn't. In fact, after listening to our
objections, he went even further and said, 'It's a dog!'

"Well, we refused to believe him. We took our
prototype and went to the L.A. Home Show. While
we were there we collected testimonials from people
— who wrote them on their business cards — about
how wonderful our Handi-Susan was. The results
were encouraging enough so that we went ahead. We
took out a full page in *Popular Mechanics*. We shipped
samples off to construction companies and real estate
developers who were building model homes. We even
set up a West Coast sales office in L.A. We were completely out of control. We let our imaginations run
way out in front of us, fantasizing about the company
plane we certainly were going to need. After all, it
would help us to make those transcontinental visits
we would have to make after our East Coast second
factory went on line.

"We did make a few sales. In the big stores in
New York we placed a few items on consignment. If
they sold, we were told, we could expect payment in

120 days or so. Aside from that, there was a scattered interest here and there, but in the end we sold about 50. It became clear that the manufacturer knew what he was talking about. Our product was a dog. Our project was a failure. Entrepreneurs have to [be ready to] fail. Intellectually, I knew that but, nevertheless, I took it personally. Very personally. When it happened, I didn't want to look at it. I denied that anything was wrong.

"By this time drinking was becoming a real problem. I had started when I was 16, and during my young adult life, I managed to keep things under control. But when this deal in L.A. went sour, I started to drink heavily and kept it up for the next five years. Between the drinking and the denial [of drinking and the business failure], I was in a constant dream world. From this point, I started to go downhill steadily. I had trouble finding a job. I took any sales job I could find: more commission jobs, selling children's magazines door-to-door. Anything that would bring me cash right away. Still, I deluded myself into thinking that I was fine — I certainly could not admit to the alcoholism — and yet things were becoming more and more desperate. By now, my wife and I had three children, and I was just barely scraping by.

"At 35, I hit bottom. A friend who had stopped drinking a few years earlier had become very involved in AA. He suggested to me that I go to one of their meetings. At first, I wouldn't even consider it. The part of me that refused to believe that I was an alcoholic saw no reason to go. The rest of me was scared to death. But one night I just gave up. I will never forget that evening. It was raining. I was wearing second-hand clothes and an old pair of Hush Puppies. I felt that this was the end of my life. I felt like a complete failure.

"Without my knowledge, my AA friend had called ahead and told them to be on the lookout for a red-haired guy named Fred. So, when I walked in the door that night, I was greeted by someone who said to me 'Are you Fred? Come in, we've been waiting for you.'

"I can't describe how that made me feel. There was a sense of failure. I felt ashamed. Sad. And yet at the same time, I also felt completely welcome and at home at that meeting. And, as is so common in situations like this, when the AA members spoke up, I realized with a shock and with relief that I was not the only one to feel the way I was feeling. Others — a whole roomful of other men and women — had experiences that I thought only I had been through. It was like a weight was taken off my shoulders. I knew this was the place for me.

"Once I started going to AA things improved for a while. I was very committed to the fellowship and became involved in all sorts of activities, both with old members and with new ones. I stopped drinking and, gradually, over a period of months, put myself back together. After a while, I even started selling real estate again.

"Within a couple of years I had put together and sold three land developments. Things were moving again, and I had regained much of my old self-confidence and drive. Not that my basic attitudes about life and work had changed much. In spite of the importance that AA places on handing your life over to a higher power, I still felt — just as I had learned from my father — that getting on in this world meant never trusting anyone else, going it alone. So, naturally, I placed a lot of stock in taking charge. The way to win, as far as I was concerned, was to take and keep control, then, with brains and hard work, fight your way to the top.

"Then I hit my second big crisis. A land project which had looked very promising in the beginning was thrown completely out the window when the government changed the zoning laws on us. I couldn't believe it. Here I was; I had overcome an enormous problem with alcoholism. My life was once again beginning to show a little promise. I had this land development company and a construction company, a nice big house in a good part of town, and, wham, I was hit out of nowhere. It took me completely by surprise. Frantically, I worked and worked and worked to try to find some way of saving this project. But, almost overnight, I had been wiped out.

"The bank called me in. I had been overdrawn for some time, and I went to meet with them hoping that they would give me a little more time to work things out. I can't remember very much of that meeting now, but I do recall trying to prove to him that I had a plan that would turn things around. I was putting it all down for him on a yellow legal pad, and as I was doing so, my writing just started to go off the page. I sat back in my chair to pull myself together and fell right out of it onto the floor. The banker looked me over and told me I had better go home. 'You don't look so good,' he said. On the way out of his office, I slammed my shoulder into the door frame. I was going to pieces. My motor skills were shot. I was completely disoriented. In fact, I was having a nervous breakdown. Within a matter of months I went from putting together million-dollar business deals to doing arts and crafts in a psychiatric institution.

"Looking back on it, I believe that the breakdown was actually a blessing. Living the way I was, at that level of stress, would certainly have done me in, if I had not been stopped in my tracks. But, at the time, I had no sense of anything but complete failure. I was in the hospital for 85 days. I had repeated electro-shock therapy, and long sessions with a psychiatrist who would never say anything to me. In the middle of all this, I was discharged but I couldn't cope and had to be recommitted. This was without doubt the bleakest and most despairing time in my life, and the toll this took on my family was enormous. Once again, I thought my life was over.

"The change that marked the beginning of my long way back was a small project I did in the institution's woodworking shop. It was very simple: a breadboard made out of five pieces of wood, glued together, shaped and sanded. I remember I made a recess in the handle with the idea that I would carve my name inside, but my hand was still so unsteady that I couldn't write the letters. I turned it into a little design. There was a hole in the end with a loop of string. That was it. Nothing fancy. But I can't tell you how proud I felt of that cutting board! After all my failures, this was a success. When the hospital wood-working instructor saw it, he heaped praises on me, admiring the little recess and the design inside it, and the hole in the handle and the loop. I was ecstatic. I had accomplished something.

"Coming back meant achieving little victories, one after the other. I washed dishes for a while. I enjoyed that. Again there was that feeling of accomplishment in taking plates and pots and pans covered with food and making them clean. Then, one day, I screwed up my courage, and went for a job interview in a car lot. The advertisement was for a sales position, but as it turned out, all they really wanted was someone to hang around in the afternoon while the salesmen all went out drinking. At first, I had trouble. One day I was closing up the lot. I remember dragging the chain across the driveway to padlock it to a post on the other side. There was a moment of real panic in this, for when I got to the post I couldn't remember: 'Do I wrap the chain around the post to the left? Or to the right?' Of course, it didn't make the slightest difference, but I was absolutely terrified that I might get it wrong. At last I took a chance. I wrapped it to the left! And it was all right! Nothing happened. It was O.K. Another achievement!

"Sometime later, when the rest of the crew was out getting drunk and I was alone at the lot, a man came in to look at the cars on the showroom floor. Again, I was terrified. What if he wanted to talk to a salesman? What would I do then? As it turned out that is exactly what he did want to do. So we spoke and I showed him one or two things about the car he was interested in. Then I took what felt like a big leap into space. I asked him if he wanted to go for a test drive. He did. And when we came back, I wrote up the sale and he drove off in the car. In three months, I was outselling the firm's top salesman. I redesigned the showroom, reorganized the lot. Little victories led to bigger ones and then, suddenly, one day I was well again.

"Ever since that day I have continued to grow and become healthier, both in the way that I treat myself and in the way I live with others. I left car sales and went back into real estate. It has not been perfectly smooth sailing by any means. There have been setbacks and deals that have fallen through. But, as far as failure is concerned, I don't see my life in terms of success and failure any more. I just try to do the best I can and I expect — no, I am convinced — that everything is going as it should.

"Looking back on it now I can see very clearly that part of the reason I had that nervous breakdown was because I didn't completely learn my lesson from my experience with alcoholism. I couldn't let go. I had to be in charge. I suppose it's a faith question, really. I didn't believe that I had any choice but to do it all myself. I aspired to a certain class in society and used to look down on others who in my opinion didn't measure up. It was like a role I was playing, the mover and shaker, on his way to the top. That's where failure really played an important part. There was still a lot more for me find out about who I really was. It ended up costing me my company, home, family and ultimately my sanity. It took two major failures before I really came around.

"Now I see things a lot differently. I'm more interested in people — all kinds of people. I've become more accepting and less of a snob. At one time I was impressed by individuals who I thought had 'made it,' millionaires, tycoons. Now I make no distinctions among people, I'm just as interested — or more interested — in the waitress who brings me my breakfast than the high roller across the restaurant. Also, I take life more lightly and try to live for each day. I've been studying the Great Wall in China, and that has provided me with an example of how I want to live my life. For thousands of miles it winds and bends, never fighting the landscape, but following it, adjusting, accommodating, taking the irregularities in stride, so to speak.

"Most of all, I now realize that I am not in control. One of the things that AA teaches is that you have to let go, and turn over your life to a higher power. You have to take responsibility for your actions, but it's not you who really keeps things going. This has brought about big changes for me. Humility is an important value for me now. It has helped me to keep things in perspective and to lay down a foundation for growth along new and more successful lines."

Let it be said first, about Fred's story, that this is not a book about alcoholism. Sad as it is to hear an account in which alcoholism plays a big part, for our purposes the specific disease is incidental. It might as well have been some other kind of addiction or unhealthy behavior that grew out of the stress inherent in his failure experience. The alcoholism complicated and intensified his problem, of course, but our concern here is with what Fred did about his *failures* per se — specifically, in the period after the alcoholism was brought under control.

Transforming our experience of failure involves identifying and changing the deception within ourself that results in failure. Fred was deceived in his belief that he needed to be in charge. Once free of that belief he was able to begin to change the course of his life. Thus, Fred's story illustrates the necessity of surrender, or "letting go," if one is to begin a meaningful transformation.

Surrendering is not defeat. Literally, it is "handing over" to life (or to God, or both: your choice) one's compulsion to be always in control. This compulsion does not serve either life in general or individual well-being in particular. It is born usually out of fear and, often, out of dysfunction. It is an indication that basic trust, which should be achieved in the process of natural development, generally in childhood, has in some way been undermined or distorted. Through the encounter with failure, this compulsion may be exposed and checked. But the failure may well need to appear truly devastating, before the courage to surrender one's drive for control can manifest itself and prevail. Small failures that can be rationalized away, may not be strong enough medicine to purge from the mind old habits of distrust, the old insistence on being a dominant leader (in the family, business, and so on). But if one can muster the courage to surrender, to admit the simple fact that things don't always work; that failure is just as natural a phenomenon as is success, then the doors to change in one's interior world (where self-esteem and judgment and forgiveness live) can be flung open. If one is open to what life has to offer, then it's "change and be changed!"

Of course, none of these changes occur instantaneously. And these developments are not always evident on the "outside." Time is always an important factor in the process of real growth, even if along the way there are rare moments of breakthrough and realizations that occur with the abruptness of a thunderclap. Therefore, an important aspect of surrendering is relaxation into the sometimes extended and almost invisible process of healing. Like a broken bone that needs first to be set and bound and then requires months to knit together, the transformation of failure will proceed largely at its own pace. And, just as one whose physical injury compels him to make allowances for a disability, so, in recovering from crisis, it is important that people care for themselves, aware that even though it may not be always apparent, healing is indeed underway.

UNIQUENESS AND SOLIDARITY

As healing and transforming changes occur in our self-understanding; when we make a positive response to failure, our self-image begins to alter. Less encumbered by habitual, limiting definitions of ourselves, we may start to see more clearly who it is we really are. We find that we are more — much more — than the sum of parts designed and stamped out by others who have their own motives for perceiving us in a limited way. We are unique, with characteristics, personality traits, talents, and abilities distinctly our own.

This uniqueness lies at the heart of our identities, of how we define ourselves. Uniqueness is what makes identity possible. As we prepared this book, we were impressed time and again by our respondents' stories of the relationship between their reestablishment of well-being and their rediscovery of uniqueness. If an individual can recover his particular sense of self, then self-worth will follow. It is only through the restoration of a positive self-image, based on concrete realities discovered in their identities, that the men and women we spoke with were able to reestablish the ability to find meaning in their experience.

At the same, it is essential that your life, your experience, is part of a much wider and greater web. It can be enormously liberating to discover — even in your own uniqueness — how much you share with all other men and women. You are a singularity, but you are not alone. You may sing a particular song no one before you has ever sung, but the singing itself and the writing of songs binds you to your fellows just as strongly as the uniqueness of your song makes you a separate individual. And so, suppose then, we think of the uniqueness of your failure: surely, in the midst of it you will feel at some bleak moment you have failed in a really unprecedented way. Yet, listen to the stories in this book, talk to your friends or family, and you will see that your experience may not be so original after all. Your bankruptcy, divorce, rejection for the prom date or for the promotion turns out to be closely comparable to the experience of others.

AUTHENTICITY

Authenticity and uniqueness are related. Authenticity is the "living-out" of uniqueness. In the process of transforming oneself through failure, this uniqueness-in-action is essential. Throughout our interviews we could trace a clear relationship between personal inauthenticity and an individual's readiness to judge events as failures, *in the face of* equally valid alternate judgments. People would feel most like failures when they felt themselves unable to live up to *another's* definition of success — not to their own.

Therefore, the first task in the process of transforming failure is to identify what in a person's history or experience has led him or her to compromise this authenticity, to discern his or her own voice among the many other clamoring voices. Once found, this voice calls the individual back to an understanding of what is personally meaningful, a center and a foundation for growth "built along more successful lines."

When, in interactions with others, one is able to act consistently out of an authentic personal center, life itself becomes authentic. Failure cannot take root. Remember, failure is a *judgment* we pass on our experience. It is not the only judgment available to us. Although events and relationships in our lives may affect us to the point where it is difficult to take an alternate view, we are always free to call the experience by another name. When we do not, it may be because some element of deception, some half-truth, in our understanding of ourselves or our experience, sets us up to see and choose the negative. The importance of this cannot be underestimated for, to a very large extent, we are shaped by the thoughts and feelings we carry around with us.

The stories in this book bear this out. In my own case, spelled out in detail in the Appendix, I felt that I had failed because I accepted a set of assumptions about success that had been prepared for me by my culture and which I uncritically applied to myself. Jim, "the ad man," failed when he aspired to become a career type he had encountered in a Hollywood movie. Vicky failed at the art gallery when she allowed herself to be swept up by the fast-track mentality of her peers. Jonathan failed through a false assumption that his options were circumscribed by traditional career paths. Anne's nearly fatal crisis arose from the loss of herself to the expectations of her mentors at school. In every case, where the person had chosen the word "failure" to describe his or her experience, some degree of that person's true identity had been lost or subordinated in favor of something "other," or something incomplete, trying to pose as the self — and usually smuggled in from outside the self. Their experiences of failure were, in fact, a collapse into inauthenticity.

The following is an account that may strike many as radical, not only from a political point of view, but from an existential one as well. Few people will want to push their lives to the limit in the way that is described here. In the words of Buckminster Fuller, this is "deep end all the way."

Nevertheless, we include it, because it clearly illustrates what is possible if an experimental attitude to life is combined with a refusal to compromise one's authenticity. Failure is given a real run for its money.

LEWIS'S STORY

Lewis Randa (real name) is a bearded Italian dervish. He is in his early 40s, energetic to the brink of hyperactivity, and speaks with intensity and mirth, undergirded by a strong sense of conviction. Lewis has made a career of seeing the promise and blessings that "failure" can bring. In 1973, he founded in Sherborn, Massachusetts, an unusual school for handicapped students, now highly acclaimed. Since then, the Life Experience School has been joined by the Peace Abbey, also located in Sherborn, an interfaith center for peace activism worldwide. At the school, Lewis involves the students in his commitment to world peace through the interpersonal relationships that are fostered, the curriculum, and by including them in activism around issues that are important to them. The work of the school and the Peace Abbey has crossed barriers of ability/disability and local/world action. Here he shares a story of how he started on his life's path, including various failures *en route*, and of a theoretical model he discovered, "crooked stuff."

> "I was in college in the 1960s, and I don't know if I can begin to explain to you how significant the antiwar movement was to me, except to say that it permeated my entire life. The crisis that led up to my experience in the military, started with the deaths of Martin Luther King and Bobby Kennedy, both of whom were teaching peace, and both of whom were

violently gunned down. I had been very active on my campus in Bobby's campaign. I coordinated the campaign at the University of Iowa, and then I was flown to the University of Nebraska to set up their campaign. That was really wonderful because it was the first time I had ever flown in a plane, and then I met Bobby Kennedy at the hotel and had my very first Coors [beer] with him! His compassionate commitment to people aroused in me a real desire to serve. He said 'We can change the world, we can make a difference' — almost inane notions, but they were well implanted in my soul.

"So I spent most of my senior year working on the campaign and feeling so hopeful about the promise of the future. When he was shot I was bereft. My spiritual, emotional, and philosophical rug was pulled out from under me, and I felt exposed and lost. Then what happens? Hubert Humphrey got the nomination. Nixon became president. And the people I believed in the most got killed. I wondered if the teachings of Christ were failing, if the teachings of Gandhi didn't work, whether the dreams of my generation were simply foolish. I was at sea.

"Of course, this was also during Vietnam, and once I was out of college I was fair game for the draft. My father suggested that I enter the National Guard; that way I could pursue my career in special education, and just be a weekend warrior. I was naive enough to think I could swallow this bitter pill and just get through it. But, of course, in boot camp, we were no longer just passively accepting the violence in our society, we were being actively trained for it! All my values were being confronted. The question was: 'Are you going to buy into this? Are you going to betray everything you believe in?' Well, I wasn't sure. I started by bringing records of Bobby Kennedy's and Martin Luther King's speeches to boot camp. I had a little record player, and I would sit on my bunk and listen to them. Of course, everybody thought I was losing it. They thought I was in massive denial — that I hadn't figured out that my heroes were dead (and, by extension, their teachings). So fine, already I seemed strange to them.

"I could deal with the regimentation of boot camp, I could handle the physical training, but I hit the wall when it came to rifle practice. I was given an M16 rifle and sent out to a rifle range and there was this row of silhouettes of human beings. You start shooting at them. And you know, when you get a bullseye you get points! It becomes interesting, a bit of a challenge. And as I got the hang of it, there was a moment when it was . . . fun? That freaked me out. All of a sudden it was like those video games or Nintendo — if you abstract it enough then you can, just like they did in Iraq [in 1991], start dropping bombs on 'targets,' not people. So, on the one hand, there was a sense that I couldn't measure up, but on the other, a repugnance that I could be good at this . . . I did measure up! That scared me even more. I had to decide — I had to become clear on what I intuitively felt was right, and do it. On an intellectual level it was easy enough to say, 'It's only eight weeks. Just get through it.' But my inner voice kept saying, 'You could do that, but you're nothing more than your conscience.' That was the most important part, mainly because these two guys got killed for teaching what I believe. So all of a sudden — more important than acceptance, more important than money, more important than prestige — I was coming to terms with this tension between what I was expected to do, and what I knew was right.

"So I started on the path of society's definition of 'failure' starting with the military, in a BIG way. It was GREAT! I failed the rifle range because I refused to take my gun. I failed to rise up through the ranks because I refused the move up. I couldn't even explain what I was doing, I just knew I couldn't move up from E1 to E2 and feel good about it. Then I refused the pay. At the time I hadn't even heard about conscientious objection, so I really wondered if there was something weird about me. The others wondered if maybe I was gay (although I was pretty clear on that score), but I remember feeling that I had to do this, although I was constantly questioning myself the whole way along. And it's so hard to be on the outside of things, it goes against the grain of what's comfortable for people. You're told to 'fall in' and you stand in line at attention and they call your name to come take your weapon card. But if you refuse to take your weapon card, they call you up front by yourself and begin belittling you, and that's where the challenge comes in. You yearn to GET BACK into that line, to take the tension off.

"Once I became clear that I couldn't 'fall in,' then fasting became the tool. I needed to change my physiological self — not just my psychological attitude to what was going on — I had to experience a dramatic shift within me that would make my internal beliefs externally evident. Gandhi taught about the powers of fasting, so I started to fast. Now I had even more completely separated myself from the group — here's somebody who's not digesting anything, when the rest of the group is. I don't know if I could have done it without the fast. You know, if you eat with everybody you kind of buy into the social ritual of the battalion, and you get comfortable, and a little lethargic after a big meal, then eventually you're part of it all. As soon as I stopped eating with them I broke from it. This was in the summer and I was on a 15-day stint, so I knew I had 15 days to prove a point. At first I stopped eating, but after about nine days I realized I'd have to stop drinking water as well, otherwise I'd just be discharged and go back to work having lost a lot of weight, but having accomplished nothing. So for the last five days I also stopped drinking water yet kept up with the rest of the activities, and pretty soon I collapsed. They told me to get up and I couldn't, so they carted me off to the hospital. And sent me to a shrink. But you have to picture this — there wasn't anywhere for him to interview me except for the dentist's office, so here I am sitting in a dental chair being presented with phrases like 'people who live in glass houses shouldn't throw stones — what does that mean?' So we talked for a while, he asked me why I wasn't eating and I explained why I felt that I couldn't eat, and he gave me a series of questions to respond to, and at the end he wrote in my file, 'obsessed with peace.' That was my diagnosis — 'obsessed with peace'! And he recommended that I be immediately discharged, and said that the military would be held responsible because I was willing to fast to the point of inflicting permanent damage on myself.

"Throughout this whole event I was constantly grilling myself: 'Is this the right thing to do? Am I crazy? Am I egocentric? What am I doing this for?' And I kept coming back to my mentors, who were willing to risk it all for their beliefs. If a general sends you into battle, you follow. These ideals sent me into an inward battle.

"I think I needed this battle. I needed to come to terms with the failure of two of my heroes to complete their lives, and I needed to move on to what I was to do with my life. I was translating all of these negative experiences into ingredients for the kind of heart and mind that could create an alternative model for something. So I had to do my own thing, and having faced off with the military, I totally believed in my ability to live by my beliefs — not that I already knew how, but that I had it within me to develop.

"So this led me into establishing an alternative model for special education, the Life Experience School. We're constantly having visitors come to spend the day with us and the kids, and they are so amazed by the love and happiness and wholeness they find here. And my search for alternative visions led me along all the winding roads that ended in the creation of the Peace Abbey and all the exciting work that's coming out of this place.

"During my experience with the military, I discovered that it was helpful for me to think of difficult experiences as being good for me. I started to become aware of the power of re-languaging things. I couldn't be comfortable with the idea of 'a silver lining' — I needed to create my own metaphor. To live effectively with the problems of life you have to create new, vital, and authentically-you metaphors. That's what I'm good at. So I began to 'reframe' my experiences — good and bad — and discovered that the conflict became fun. In fact, I found I was more successful at that than when things go right. To this day, when I see things going wrong I know I'll be at my best, because I can see into and through the problems and my ego doesn't get caught up in them nearly as much as it did a couple of decades ago. It's as though in times of difficulty instead of the transmission over-winding, I've been blessed to have a fifth gear, and once I get into fifth, everything gets translated — framed — differently. I see new possibilities where they didn't exist before, and I can dive into the process of discovering what's unfolding here. And that's very important — the focus on process. It's always the process. That's one thing Bobby and Martin taught me: don't go for the end product. They never reached their ultimate goals, everything leading up from that, and away from that, was simply process. Getting there isn't the point — it's the journey.

"One of the students at the Life Experience School helped me to clarify what I mean by seeing the opportunities in what looks like a bad situation. One day we were waiting for gas at the station, and Kari, a 15-year-old girl, said to me, 'Lewis, you always talk about what you put out, you get back. Well, I've been doing this volunteer work in the nursing home, and I've been trying to be extra nice but people yell at me. And that's only one example — lots of times I try to do something right and it comes back wrong.' So I said, 'Kari, when you get up in the morning and your favorite clothes are all ironed and laid out on the bed for you, and the cab comes on time to bring you to school, and you have a great day and see everybody you like, and you have the lunch you want, and when you get home the movie you want to see is on TV and your sister is away so you get to watch it, and at dinner the meal is exactly when you want and you go

to bed ... and it's a perfect day? Well, those are the
days that really don't allow opportunity to come forward because it was exactly the way you planned it
and wanted it to happen. But if you think of it as a
straight stick, and one end of the day is point A and
the other is point B, and you're standing at point A
and you want to get to point B (the end of a perfect
day), and you throw the stick — your conscious mind
wants your life to work out so that you go straight to
point B. But we know life doesn't work that way —
there are all kinds of problems, mistakes are made,
and you just have to live with it. Everything is made
up of positives and negatives, and you can't have one
without the other. So I want you to think of that
straight stick as having a crook in it — bend it a little
bit. And the bend is some unwanted situation or event,
and the tip of that stick starts at A, but it's not going
to B. It's going to C. But you don't know where C is
because it goes around the corner and you can't see
around the corner. So you've got to trust that not only
is something there, but there's promise in it. Think of
it like a boomerang — what you put out, you do get
back. But the reason the boomerang comes back to
you is because it has that crook in it, and that crook
represents the difficulties and problems in life. So,
'What you put out, you get back,' means that life gives
you back what you need, based on all the problems
and opportunities of life. Now you can see that the
problems are not only your companion, but your co-
creators of what you need. Instead of calling them
problems, call them 'crooked stuff,' and watch for
what comes back.'

"Failure is a grace-laden opportunity. I think it
requires faith to believe that in the course of every

> day you are offered opportunities to have your needs
> met, and I think it requires gratitude to acknowledge
> what you already have. And to the extent that you
> can appreciate what you have — even if it feels small
> compared to what feels like a mountain of problems
> — then you see that doors are opening, and you can
> begin to make your way day by day."

As a society we may be a long way from adopting the
"thankfulness" and openness to life that Lewis Randa considers an operating principle. At the same time, such an
attitude is close to the scientific or experimental approach
described by Parker Palmer in one of the epigraphs at the
beginning of this chapter. If one can observe what life brings
and accept it — at least provisionally — as an experience
that contributes to an open-ended future, then one is empowered to find meaning and opportunity in situations that
for others might seem irredeemable disasters. This is what
Lewis means, we believe, by his homemade image,
"crooked stuff." Those who see their own development as
finished and over with will have difficulty in adopting this
positive attitude toward the failure. Those who know they
are still students of life with much to learn — no matter
what age they have attained or how much experience they
have accumulated — they will reap the rewards of failure —
not without pain — but with a surprising degree of satisfaction.

Community: The Context for Success

It may be argued that the emphasis we have placed on
personal authenticity is merely another repackaging of the
classic American myth of individualism. Certainly, there is

a way in which the ideas in this book could lead in that direction. But this would be a distortion of an important awareness common to many of the women and men we interviewed. Their crises — which may have involved a period of withdrawal from society — eventually restored them to a quality of life not present before. These are not the "solitary singers" who populate so much of our serious literature (Whitman, Thoreau, and a host of others) and our popular culture (the cowboy, the Lone Ranger). Instead, these people tend to be those who by hook or by crook (and often with the *help* of failure) have become admirable coworkers, good partners in marriage and family, reliable neighbors, and sensitive citizens: though at times they all felt deeply isolated in their failures, they passed through to living a much more deeply *connected* life.

This connectedness may take many forms. In some cases, individuals were inspired to make a major change, such as a career move into one of the helping professions. Others began to cultivate an interest in social or political issues or causes that were previously outside their circle of concern. Common to all was a renewed interest in the quality of their relationships, old and new. People talked of having more patience with others and a deeper sense of concern and empathy. A quality of generosity was also common, immediately evident to us in their eagerness to pass along what they had learned about failure, either through thoughtful and thorough completion of our questionnaires or through hours spent with us on the telephone.

It is true that in the majority of cases these responses included — implicitly or explicitly — some social critique. Occasionally, this was directed at society as a whole. In other cases, the mores and values of a particular class or sub-culture, or of the ways in which families and individuals behave within such groups, were identified as sources of difficulty. As we discussed in Chapter Two, there are indeed patterns of behavior and ways of thinking in any society that may obstruct and distort an individual's self-awareness. Someone thus affected will have trouble not only in coming to terms with himself and in entering into relationships with others, but will also have difficulty finding ways to participate in the world that are relevant to his personal identity, meaningful with regard to his values and concerns, and satisfying in the employment of personal gifts and interests.

Therefore, we are presented with a paradox. The critiques developed by these individuals and the means by which they sought to transform their experience are anti-social only to the extent that they are pro-community, if by "community" we mean a fabric of relationships among individuals who seek to promote each other's well-being. Such a community has no stake in customs or practices that lead to inauthenticity. Such a community is not rigidly defined, nor does it seek to place unnecessary constraints upon the individual. In return, individuals see that their growth and well-being is directly related to their participation in that community.

So where does all this lead?

SUCCESS

Perhaps this leads us to begin to shape a new understanding of success.

First of all, success is surely more than that-which-is-not-failure. Success can include failure. Success is a way of life based on a commitment to making choices that come from an authentic personal center, "living by your own lights." Therefore, it means taking a stand in the midst of your experience, meeting what life brings and — good or bad — learning from the experience. Success is not solitary, it is bound up with the struggles and aspirations of those with whom "we live and move and have our being." Success is meaningless if it isolates us from the world, because life in the world — and its web of relationships — is the only context where meaning may become a possibility.

The higher up you go, the more mistakes you're allowed. Right at the top, if you make enough of them it's considered to be your style.

FRED ASTAIRE

When such as I cast out remorse
So great a sweetness flows
into the breast
We must laugh and
we must sing,
We are blest by everything,
Everything we look upon is blest.

WILLIAM BUTLER YEATS

APPENDIX

THE AUTHOR'S STORY
John Lord

Fall down seven times. Stand up eight.

JAPANESE PROVERB

And the end of the journey shall be to arrive where we started and know the place for the first time.

T. S. ELIOT

THE JOURNEY THROUGH LIFE is in many ways like any other sort of excursion. The sudden delays and the surprises, good and bad, the help you get from those you never expected to care, and the indifference of those you did, these are experiences that are common to any sort of travel. Additionally, the route that one takes through life may be more guessed at than known for certain, and one may find at several points that one is not at all where one intended to be. Then come the agonizing decisions: do I go back to the point where I lost the trail? Or do I forge ahead and hope that things will turn out nonetheless?

These are the sorts of things that everyone's stories have in common. Education, family of origin, culture of origin, and so on, are all extremely important. They help to shape us and, consequently, help to shape our responses to what living hurls onto our path. At the heart of things, however, lies a shared experience of life that is universal, that only takes on meaning when it comes to grips with what is ultimately important. Because of this universality, my own story, including my failure, which is in its own way odd, peculiar and extreme, will I hope have things within it which others may recognize.

I was born in New York City in 1954. Soon after, my family moved to Riverside, Connecticut, and from there to Greenwich, into the only house I can remember living in as a child. My father was — and still is — an attorney, and the son and grandson of career military men from the state of Maine and their straitlaced Edwardian wives. He had graduated from Harvard Law School, become an associate in a downtown maritime law practice, worked his way to the top, and has never left. Needless to say, his views on how one gets ahead in the world typify what has come to be called the "old paradigm." Intelligence, savoir faire, stability, hard work and sacrifice were the primary virtues. Competition, an unalterable fact of life. Inclusion into society's elite the reward. From his perspective, the concept of elitism has little negative connotation. It implied being part of that group of men (usually) who had proven themselves capable and deserving of exercising influence in matters of state or in the world of business. Closer to home, my father's work ethic meant financial security for his family, opportunities for us to travel, and to spend summer vacations away from Greenwich. Every year, my mother and my siblings would go to the coast of Maine to a fishing village near where he, too, had spent his childhood summers.

My mother took upon herself the responsibilities that attend the running of a household in suburban America. There were four children in my family: an elder brother, a younger sister, and a much younger brother who was born when I was in fifth grade. There was much to look after and she managed very well. In addition to the usual running around between one school event or another, she made a great effort to expose us to the museums and theaters of nearby Manhattan. This was to have a real impact on me, perhaps more than on the others. By the time I was in junior high, I had already developed a strong interest in antiquity — ancient Rome and the Middle Ages — and in the performing arts.

Greenwich is pretty nearly what it's cracked up to be. A very rich town, lovely, stately, well manicured, virtually all-white, largely Protestant, conservative, with plenty of huge houses, conspicuous consumption, country clubs, and shops that most of the world couldn't buy a toothpick in. In addition, there was more than enough of good manners, artificial friendliness, and emotional alienation and alcoholism to go around. There was also a sense that the town was a cultural oasis in an unenlightened world. There is a story that at one time the town was considered as a possible location for the United Nations, but the residents turned it down fearing that it would spoil the neighborhood. That pretty much says it all.

I hated Greenwich, detesting everything about the town with all the intensity and passion of childhood. School life for me was purgatory on good days and hell on bad days. I began at Brunswick School which I attended up through the fifth grade. It was there I discovered my love of music and my hatred of athletics. Everything else — beside the rather too frequently verbally abusive teachers — is only dimly remembered.

In fifth grade I transferred to Greenwich Country Day School. My memories of that school are not at all dim. Compared to Brunswick, GCDS was like the moment when the dentist's drill bites deeper than the reach of the novocaine. A few well-meaning people I met there made it possible for me to survive. At any rate, while at GCDS, I did discover that I was reasonably good at acting, which, combined with an interest in photography, sealed my fate socially in a school that measured everything by one's performance in competitive team sports.

Looking back on it now it is so clear how early the indoctrination begins: competition is the pathway to achievement recalling so closely the phrase by Lord Frazier: "The Battle of Waterloo was won on the playing fields of Eton." Victorian Anglo-Saxon cosmology and polemics. Never mind that if the playing fields of Eton and other places like it had never existed, there might not have been a Battle of Waterloo in the first place! That sort of thinking was nowhere in evidence. I do not recall a single genuinely cooperative activity at any time in my schooling.

But in the summer all this changed. In the summer I would leave Connecticut with my family and spend July and August in a grey shingled cottage on the coast of Maine so close to the water's edge that a high tide and a full moon would bring the waves within a pebble's toss of my window. My recollection of childhood in Maine is, I know well, reconstructed with the favorable disposition given to such places of safety as we look back on them. There were occasions of unhappiness, certainly. I didn't enjoy sailing class (I was too fat to be much good in a small boat), and there was a family of ferociously territorial bullies a few cottages down. Nevertheless, nothing could have been further from the misery of my school life. When I was in Maine, I was happy. I was out from under.

In Maine, my imagination had free rein. The woods became forts or cities or towns or haunted groves. The lighthouse was a castle and the rocks a high sierra or a desert island. Rowboats became Viking ships and the outboard motorboat a destroyer. There were stretches of coast to explore, and often we would be gone half the day. Or we would sit hour after hour on the beach hurling stones at some makeshift target slowly being towed away by the tide. In the evening, the cottage came alive with people young and old, and I remember these nights as the best hours of my boyhood. There would be accounts of adventures in parts of the world so obscure or remote I couldn't even find them on a map. Word games inside and "flashlight death" outside. But best of all, before bedtime, there would be the reading of stories — and such stories — by the fire. *The Chronicles of Narnia* by C. S. Lewis, *The Hobbit* and *The Lord of the Rings* by J. R. R. Tolkien. These books became my first experience with fantasy and myth. Though I did not know it at the time, they were also my first encounter with the themes of scripture and the spiritual traditions of the West.

Of all the many happy experiences that I can recall, there was one which I now see as especially important in the way my life was later to develop. It was a spiritual — even mystical — experience, and although there was a time when I might not have seen this as relevant to issues of work, vocation, and *failure*, I now see it as central. Also, there was a time when I thought such things were rare, but now I have a hunch that this too is not the case. In fact, I believe that each one of us could find in our own experience just such an event, but the patterns of daily life and ficiality of our culture drive them from memory. As poet Robert Bly conceives it, they become part of the contents of a bag that each of us drags behind us, full of parts of our identity and our experience — shameful and joyful — that we have repressed because they do not correspond to the persona we have adopted or have been forced to adopt and through which we address the world. Bly calls the material in the bag our "human shadow."[1]

There was one night among the many warm and clear nights of midsummer, when I decided to go out alone to the end of the pier that jutted out from the rocks and seaweed in front of the cottage. It was a night of brilliant stars that seemed close enough to gather up by the armful. I sat down at the end and listened to the voice of the wind in the pines and let my legs dangle over the edge. I tucked my elbows up onto the low railing and peered out past the gently tossing sailboats tethered at their moorings and the bobbing pot buoys and, farther off, the lighthouse, reefs and islands nearly covered now by the night. I can still feel that warm wind upon my face and the rough surface of the weathered board beneath my thighs. Clearest of all was the sense of expectation. I felt as if I had been called out to watch the secret rendezvous of the stars and the sea, and I felt as if God knew I was there.

And then, for one unforgettable instant, there was no sea, there were no stars, there was no dock, there was no me. All boundaries, all separateness fell away and flew up into the sky like a loon. I was part of everything and everything was part of me. It struck me. I will say it struck me. But I was not afraid. Indeed, now as I look back on that night I see that fear would have been impossible because fear depends on disunion and in that moment all was one.

I have no memory now of what I did after that instant

set me back down upon the earth. I expect that I rejoined whatever activity was in progress back on land. I do know that soon after I realized that this night had marked off something of the deepest significance for me. I did not know whether this was a beginning or an end. I had certainly never experienced anything of the kind before, but for some reason, I quickly assumed that this was not an experience that could be repeated in later life. I was quite sure that — as an adult — I would lose the capacity for such an event. For years I regarded that night as the last night of my childhood.

Today I understand that — disregarding the dismissive arguments from certain schools of psychology — this was a moment of revelation. It did not have a "meaning" per se. It was an experience of meaning itself. Such things are difficult to discuss because they involve ways of knowing that are beyond the intellectual, but the fact that I never completely forgot it contributed to my incessant restlessness with any activity that was superficial or narrow or did not have some reference to the feeling of wholeness I experienced that night. Sometime later I came across the following comment by C. S. Lewis concerning the view of the universe held in the Middle Ages. It was a view based upon a divine order markedly different from our understanding today.

You must go out on a starry night and walk about for half an hour trying to see the sky in terms of the old cosmology. Remember that you now have absolute Up and Down. The earth is really the center, really the lowest place; movement to it from whatever direction is downward movement. As a modern, you located the stars at a great distance. For distance you must now substitute that very special, and far less abstract, sort of distance which we call height. To look out on the night sky with modern

eyes is like looking out over a sea that fades away into the mist,
or looking about one in a trackless forest — trees forever and no
horizon. To look up at the towering medieval universe is much
more like looking at a great building. [2]

The old cosmology — which obviously is a mythic
and not a scientific view — still has the greatest meaning
for me. But these were inchoate thoughts that were to stay
with me, mostly invisibly, and only come to life when failure after failure had begun to strip my illusions away.

At the end of my ninth grade year I was sent off to
boarding school. This chapter of my story had an inauspi-
cious beginning: before arriving I received a letter from the
football coach inviting me to come to school early to attend
football tryouts. It was important that I make this effort,
because, as his letter assured me, "if you can't win on Saturday, you can't win in life." I didn't show up.

The succeeding transitions in my life came upon me
as though I were a passenger on a train, driven by someone
I could not see and did not know. Seasons and semesters
glided by half-observed without significance. These were
just stations where the train did not stop. My memories of
these years of high school and college are fragmentary and
episodic. Lurching and jolting from one grade to the next,
or from one school to the next, I had little idea of where
this was all leading.

Boarding school was a crazy stew of adolescent hormones, distracted draft-dodging professors, anti-Vietnam
War activity, leftists, neo-Nazis, my first non-white friend,
the mauling of girls from the boarding school down the
hill, cigarettes, recreational drugs and alcohol. I continued
my interest in the theater. I studied as little as possible,
played the guitar as much as possible. I never actually
failed, at least not in an academic sense. From an existen-

tial standpoint, however, my failure was already well under way. Estranged from myself, passive in the conduct of
my life, I was moving farther and farther away from any
sense of who I was or what I was supposed to do.

Next was Bowdoin College in Brunswick, Maine. My
feelings about Bowdoin are entirely different. I, myself, was
ponderous and arrogant, still in deepest, darkest adolescence. Having failed to accompany myself through this period in my life, I was relentless in my pursuit of relationships that could fill the void. If a woman expressed even a
passing interest in me — and often even if she hadn't — I
was delirious, intoxicated, sure that this person — this
one and only person — could make my life happy and
meaningful. Of course, there were very few who would
tolerate such maniacal behavior, and I went through what
seemed an endless cycle of ecstasy and despair.

Academically, I gained little of what I should have
received out of the college experience. I have heard it said
that "Education is wasted on the young." That describes
my experience in college, and to this day it is a real source
of regret. Bowdoin was a wonderful opportunity for me to
learn from some of the very best minds in education anywhere, but I was just clever enough to do reasonably well
with practically no work. I majored in Greek and Latin,
which was at least in part a gesture of defiance of the
growing utilitarianism among my contemporaries. But my
teachers were wonderful and managed, in spite of my de-
liberate indifference, to kindle a real interest in me in the
classics and ancient civilization.

During my junior year I went to London, which was
in many ways a pivotal experience in my life. London was
not altogether foreign. After all, many of the people in my
home town behaved as though they felt the wrong side
had won the American Revolutionary War, but London

was different enough to enable me to get some perspective on my life. And, of course, London was cosmopolitan. In my neighborhood there were Arabs and Argentineans and Aussies and Americans. Furthermore, I made a few friendships through which I regained my long absent sense of humor. While in London, I continued to pursue my involvement in the theater and started to develop some little interest in literature. It was a wonderful year — full of romance and adventure and after-hours pints, and jaunts through back streets, and long talks and longer silences, and short sweet fond affairs. When I landed at JFK airport at the end of the summer, the only thing on my mind was how soon I could get back.

My senior year at Bowdoin was marred somewhat by a full length cast on my leg. In the last part of August, just days before the end of vacation, the car I was riding in was broad-sided at high speed. The driver — one of my closest friends from college — was seriously injured with damage to the stem of his brain. He was in a coma for weeks, and very nearly didn't make it. I had a nasty complex break in the middle of my right shin, and by the time I returned to school I was just beginning to be able to get around. It was a very strange final year. At a time when everyone I knew was planning feverishly for the future, I looked ahead and saw nothing. I remember feeling a distinct aversion to the usual sorts of things: law school, business school. I don't remember what I thought I was going to do, but one day, while rehearsing the part of Toby Belch in *Twelfth Night* (type casting?), I saw a poster for a drama school in a neighborhood on the outskirts of London. This was it! My chance to go back.

Drama school was very hard work. On top of that it was crazy. There were 40 or so students — some from the US and Canada — the rest from the UK. The schedule was intense, we were in close quarters, so that there was no escaping each other throughout the year. For all that, the teaching was excellent and level of commitment among the students high. Hard as it was, I remember this year as one of personal exploration into the worlds of art and literature and culture, which awakened in me a love of language, of the power of words. I decided that when I returned to the US, I would start my own theater company.

It was also my great good fortune — two weeks before the end of the year — to convince a lovely Canadian actress named Jennifer Walker to go out with me. We had been friends all year, and I had admired her craftsmanship and her professionalism, but I had never been especially attracted to her. Our last assignment was a series of scenes from various Shakespeare plays that were knit together into what might be called an Elizabethan revue. In one of these, I was cast as Romeo (casting against type, this time!) and she was cast as Juliet. That was it. We were married a little over a year later.

I returned to the US, went back to Greenwich and, with the help of a friend I imported from England, started a theater company called the Calliope Players. Our first production was a type of play that is done in England around the Christmas holidays called a pantomime. This is not the same as the silent "miming" we usually think of when we hear the word. This was a musical farce with a huge cast that collapsed under its own weight. It was not a promising start. After that things improved. We brought in professional actors from New York and produced shows from the classical repertoire, musical revues, one-act comedies, Christmas pageants, Shakespeare-in-the-park, you name it. Although I cannot be completely objective, I think that for the most part we did excellent work. Like drama school, our lives were emotionally intense, a complex of intersecting relationships, that alternately brought out in us the best and the very worst. Speaking personally, I did things I never thought I was capable of doing — good and bad. We had a core of actors and a small army of helpers from the local high school who gave new meaning to the word "trouper." Everyone made enormous personal commitments, but after a few years we exhausted the little money we had and we decided to close it down.

Although, the company was an artistic success, it failed financially. This to me was a shock and a let-down. I had never really failed at anything before — I had always been able to pull things off at the last minute. But this had not worked. I felt ashamed. Greenwich was not a town where you are supposed to fail at anything! Greenwich is to success what the Vatican is to Catholicism. If you fail here, you're a heretic; better get out of town.

It was years before I was able to recognize that the work we had done was good enough for us all to have been proud. These should have been happy memories. Now I see how valuable it would have been for me if I had given myself a few months to think — and feel — my way through this failure experience before moving on to something else. I might have saved myself a lot of trouble. Instead, we moved too quickly out of Greenwich to Boston, found jobs and began again.

Not much gelled for us in Boston, and we didn't stay there long. Jennifer and I had been in touch with a theater company in western Massachusetts, where we were hired to do public relations and audience development. I will never forget the night we arrived for our interview. It was, literally, a dark and stormy night at the end of a bleak and cold November. The company was based in an immense Gilded Age mansion that was, at that time, in an advanced state of dilapidation. We pulled into the driveway, turned off our headlights, and found ourselves completely in the dark. The huge building loomed in front of us like an eerie set piece. Leaving the car, we walked around the building trying to decide how to get in. Finding a small back door open, we walked up a creaking set of wooden stairs that opened onto a cavernous, echoing and pitch-black corridor. At the far end, a little dirty yellow light spilled out from beneath a closed door. Somewhere, music was playing. We walked down that hallway and slowly opened the door. There was the smell of marijuana and we located the source of the music, but that was all. Having nothing else to do, we sat down. Twenty minutes later we heard footsteps, far away at first but then coming closer. We did have an appointment, we really did, but at that moment we felt as though we had stumbled uninvited into a haunted mansion and half expected to see Norman Bates come around the corner. What did come around the corner was only slightly less frightening. A large and lumbering man with a shaved head appeared in the doorway. He was wearing an old army jacket and blue jeans, and I could tell from his expression that he was as surprised to see us as we were to see him. This was our introduction to a new place of employment.

I won't go into detail about this establishment. It was part commune and part personality cult. The artistic director and a few of the others were EST enthusiasts, a prejudice which they applied to their management technique. The artistic work they did was good, but as a community it was a sad and troubled place. When they ran out of money at the end of the season for which we were employed, our contract was terminated and we were left wondering what to do next. This is not to say that we didn't feel a certain relief in being free of the place. I distinctly remember feeling that laying us off prevented us from going through the difficult process of resigning. And, of course, there was, again, that feeling of shame. In some ways I felt that I had failed because for me at that time, success meant staying at something, producing results that were in some sense identifiable as successful and working my way up through the organization. None of that occurred here. Furthermore, my sense of shame was made worse by a new worry: was this losing of jobs going to be a pattern? My other friends were getting on with things: buying new cars, talking about career moves, working in lucrative positions overseas. What had I to show for all my effort?

By this time, Jennifer and I had fallen in love with the hills of western Massachusetts. We rented a small house on a hillside. There was a vegetable garden out back, and cows in the field across the road. But this area was never our land of opportunity. There were few employers and fewer jobs that appealed to us, so we decided to work for ourselves. Over the last several years we had gained a certain amount of proficiency in putting together marketing materials and had established in that area a network of artists and printers. So what did we do? What else? We started a stationery company. We called the new enterprise "Chimo," Eskimo for "hello." We produced small boxed sets of greeting cards featuring the work of local artists. Restrained by lack of funds, we stuck with monochrome designs, but the drawings were varied and included both a selection of country scenes and a set of humorous caricatures. We sold some through mail order, which never really took off. The rest we piled into the back of our beat-up Peugeot and peddled throughout New England.

We covered many miles and spoke to many retailers and sold a good many boxes of stationery. But the choice of one-color printing was a mistake, the line was too small, and we were wearing ourselves out with all the traveling. We were in a motel somewhere in Connecticut when I woke up to hear that John Lennon had been killed. Lennon was a role model for me. He was a rule-breaker and an iconoclast. For me, he always represented both an unstoppable energy and the notion that the combination of good natured irreverence and raw talent could work miracles. In refusing to buy into the career paths that had been laid down for me, and by going my own way, I felt that I was breaking the rules, too. The day he died, I simply lost my belief that all things were possible. We packed it in and drove to Vancouver.

It is clear to me now that choosing the Eskimo-Canadian name "Chimo" was an indication of Jennifer's growing desire to go home, to get away from New England, where we were having such trouble finding the direction for our lives. It was evening as we drove down out of the Coastal Mountain Range and on into Vancouver. The trip had been a hurried one. We had not the money to enjoy the sights on the way across. Montreal was cold and unfriendly. Ontario seemed all pine trees and slag heaps; I was ill at ease all through the unrelentingly flat openness of the prairies. In Alberta, we counted oil wells as I used to count Volkswagens when I was a kid, and Calgary looked like an aluminum version of the Emerald City. The trip really began for us once we began to climb the Rockies. There returned to us a sense of adventure and of accomplishment as we rose above the plains and worked our way across the Continental Divide.

The year or so that passed in Vancouver marked a shift in our thinking about work. We had by this time tried several times to find jobs or to start enterprises that would take advantage of our skills and interests as we then understood them. By this time, however, we were worn out, somewhat disillusioned and ready for a change to less stressful activity. We resolved to behave like grown-ups and go out and find"'real jobs." It was our hope that by doing so we would be able to settle down and begin to enjoy the rewards of participating in the world of business.

Vancouver seemed like a wonderful place to try it. First of all, this city, which lies with snow-crested mountains on one side and the Pacific on the other, provided the perfect setting. The climate is temperate with cool summers and warm winters, and the work ethic never seemed to interfere with anyone's appreciation for what life in such a place might have to offer. There were restaurants, and theater companies, and museums and parks, and pastry shops and flower stalls and Chinese markets, and freighters and sailboats in the bay. The city was cosmopolitan. The people were, in general, hospitable and relaxed. We felt that this time we had really landed on our feet. Jennifer soon found work selling temporary office help. She did very well and moved eventually out of sales and into placement. I was hired by the personnel company that I had asked to help me find work. We had gotten off to a fast start; things looked great.

The man I worked for was an impressive individual. Not tall, but stocky and powerful, he was an immaculate and fashionable dresser who wore European suits and gold jewelry. He had a booming voice and a commanding presence, and held his employees' attention through grand gestures of sweeping generosity and violent mood swings from elation to rage. While I worked for him, I recruited men and women from a variety of industries for placements ranging from civil engineer to insurance adjuster. I even once placed a geophysicist — without ever really knowing what that was or what he would do. Any doubt I might have felt about a little thing like integrity was swept aside by my employer's assurances. Competence was what mattered to him. And competence meant making money, in whatever way was possible.

After only a year, I left. I had grown steadily more uncomfortable about my task. The money was good but I couldn't help seeing that this work was wrong from an ethical standpoint, and the compromises I was making in the use of my gifts and abilities were unsupportable. So I quit.

This was late fall. Things were moving again toward another period of change. Our anxiety about what to do next was mounting steadily. My efforts to get something going grew increasingly frantic. I set up a small importing company with a few friends, but personalities clashed and it went nowhere. The job market was deteriorating under a recession brought on by the general decline of the timber and pulp and paper industry, the cornerstone of the provincial economy. Vancouver began to pall. Almost no one we knew had children or was even thinking about children. But we were. We remembered the little house we had rented in the Berkshire Hills, and the Norman Rockwell small-town quality of life there, and realized that New England was, after all, where we wanted to raise our family. We moved out of our apartment, found someone to drive the car back across the country, and flew to the East Coast and the US.

When we arrived back in Berkshire County, I was once again pumped up. By this time, I was using my imagination and my energy like a narcotic: it kept me running and neath my difficulties: failure to commit to anything over the long pull, failure really to know who I was or what I cared about. I was on a constant high. Going. Going.

This time my plan was to buy a Mexican restaurant. I

had no money, but while we had lived in Massachusetts previously, I had come to know this particular little business well and had thought about buying it once before. There were a few people who had expressed an interest in investing and I knew that it was profitable. We began a lengthy negotiation with the owner, but, eventually, the deal fell through. We were in a difficult position. We had no money, no car (it hadn't arrived yet) and Jennifer was pregnant. I took a job in a hotel. I worked at the front desk. I was promoted and I was canned. I suspect that my employer realized that I was not willing to make the kind of total personal commitment to the business that she expected. Later, when I began to study organizational systems and leadership styles, I discovered how great the mismatch had been. For someone with even an incipient idealism about progressive management practices, democratized workplaces, empowering employer/employee relationships, and upside down organizational charts, this hotel was the wrong place to be.

At first I was devastated about being fired. My son, Ben, was less than a year old. Jennifer was only working part-time, and now I was out of a job again. There was a growing fear that we had somehow gone wrong not only with our jobs but our lives. It wasn't supposed to be this difficult. Already, I had had more jobs — employed by others or self-employed — than anyone I knew (including people three times my age), but worse still was the feeling that not only had none of these jobs worked out, none of them could have worked out. It was becoming clear that they were all wrong or I was all wrong. Whatever I did, it seemed, quickly became dissatisfying, but I didn't know why. It was as though I were repeatedly going off track without ever knowing what being "on track" might have meant for me.

At the same time the birth of my son was an event of the greatest significance. It was a fortunate, Providential — if not redemptive — experience for me that I could stay home with him for the first year or so of his life. Devoting myself in a focused and relatively undistracted way on parenting just felt right. I had discovered a vocation. Yet, while it felt right as far as I was concerned, I was also aware that such a thing, for a man, was definitely not in the script. This was clearly a departure from what others I knew were doing. I sensed that I was crossing some significant lines of demarcation: I, a man, was at home and not "at work." Consequently, I had a relationship with my child. Through my experience of fathering, I discovered emotional depths and a willingness to risk genuine relationships with others that I am not sure I would have found otherwise. The lesson I learned — which everyone encounters in one's own life as though it had never been encountered by anyone at any time before — was the power and sacredness of the parent-child relationship. It is hard for me to discuss without sentimentality and it beggars my skill with words, but it was significant. It was a sign of something greater. Something Other. Also, it recalled some other deep connection, an echo of that earlier experience of profound relatedness, felt in my own childhood on that singular night at the end of the pier.

As that year came to a close, I allowed myself to begin to grow anxious once more about work, about my "career." I still felt that I hadn't proven myself. To me this meant much the same thing it always had: making money, having toys, taking trips, and the like. I set myself up in a home-based business, marketing children's products such as toys and furniture made by New England craftspeople. The idea smacked of integrity. In some instances, I operated as an agent receiving a commission on sales. In others,

I commissioned the products myself, marked them up and sold them wholesale. At least, that was the plan. In many ways this seemed to be a good solution. I could still spend most of my time at home: I would be doing work that I thought was worthwhile; and with the combination of low overhead and a growing market, I felt confident that my commissions would soon provide me with a comfortable income. And from there I could build and build and build. In the next three years, this modest and reasonable project was to turn into a monster that very nearly devoured me, my family and our future.

About this time, we began to go back to the Congregational Church in Stockbridge. It was an old church that had originally served as a mission to the Indians. Among other notables, the well-known 18th-century revivalist Jonathan Edwards had been a pastor there before becoming president of the College of New Jersey, later Princeton University. We were very happy there. In the midst of all our difficulties we found sources of support and understanding that we had never experienced before. More importantly, we were members of a community that was concerned about questions of value and that affirmed the importance of authenticity. Through that involvement, I began to realize that there was more at stake in life than "success." More difficult to accept, and therefore, more vigorously denied, was the growing suspicion that I had fallen out of touch with myself and what it was that I was supposed to do with my life. This suspicion haunted me, but remained obscure and inarticulate for several years to come.

These, then, were the two currents that ran throughout the process of failure, now moving to its crisis. In the accelerating, dizzying, crowded, empty vortex of events, amid all the tortured decisions, mistakes, personal con-

frontations, wrecked relationships, self-betrayals and be-
trayal by others, the desire to succeed and the fear of failure laid on the lash. Driven by desire and fear, I ran dis-
tractedly in ever-tightening circles. But all the while another voice, barely discernible above the clamor, was calling me back, calling me away, and I would not listen.

Believing that my problem with business had to do
with a simple lack of expertise, I signed up for two night
courses at the local community college. Much to my surprise, I excelled in both — one of which was accounting, a
subject I had assiduously avoided as an undergraduate. A
little knowledge is a dangerous thing, and, armed with a
self-confidence to which I was not entitled, I continued to
allow my daydreams about my crafts business to expand.
In one of those courses, I met a bright, lovely and spirited
young woman who I discovered had experience as a sales
representative for a local clothing importer. Since, by now,
I was beginning to explore how I might distribute goods
from places outside the US, I was interested in her and
what she knew. We became friends. Before long, she was
working with me. Through no fault on her part, this relationship began a chain of events that I barely survived.

We discovered that a line of angora sweaters manu-
factured in Toronto had become available. Thinking that
this could provide me with the basis for my other activities, I changed the focus of my activities. I was joined by
an old friend from grade school who had become an attorney, and after drawing up an elaborate offering memoran-
dum, took in venture capital and went into business. My
role was to administer the business, my new friend would
concentrate on sales and my old friend would provide
oversight from a legal standpoint and offer advice and encouragement. Everything seemed to make sense — except
the one thing that mattered the most: I had always de-

spised the clothing business. I remember now that as a child I had always complained bitterly when I had to spend any time in a clothing store. Furthermore, I not only disliked but positively disapproved of the fashion industry and everything it represented, seeing it as nothing more than a manifestation of the superficiality and materialism of our society. All of this authentic feeling I ignored. I enjoyed the setup, the ideas, the camaraderie. I convinced myself that with my partner's expertise, my own lack of interest in the product was of no consequence.

At first, things went well. Our sales rep had come to the enterprise with a number of contacts that provided us with accounts receivable and early revenues. In addition, she was extremely knowledgeable and had tremendous style and a natural gift for sales, fashion, and design. Soon, however, things started to deteriorate. Projections had been seriously overestimated. The expense of keeping a sales rep on the road all over New England was underestimated, and I was foolishly contributing to the draining off of resources by drawing a salary myself. We lasted a mere four seasons, two years, and the company as we had conceived it was in a shambles.

I was stuck — completely stuck — or so I thought. I had taken money from family and friends I knew in the community and I frantically refused to let that business fail. Desperately, I thought up strategy after strategy to find a way out. I was spinning my wheels. By this time my working relationship with my partners was severely strained. We were unable to continue to pay our sales rep, and by mutual consent — and I think to her relief — she went on to other things. Left with what was for me a sizable bank debt, a sense of unconditional obligation to the shareholders, and 20 thousand dollars worth of inventory, I searched for an escape.

Had I allowed myself at this point to recognize that this experience was a failure, and had I learned the lessons this fiasco had to offer me about vocation, values, and personal gifts and talents (in this case misapplied), I could have saved myself great heartache, stress, and financial loss in the months ahead. Still, I was dogged in my determination to turn this situation into a success.

I resolved to open a retail store. I had hired an assistant, a talented clothing designer, who, I hoped, would fill the knowledge gap left by her predecessor. I had a vision of a fun, funky, discount shop. The first objective was to try to liquidate our inventory. I had been fascinated by what chains like Banana Republic were doing with creating a total environment for their stores. There was a quality of presentation about this approach that recalled my interest in the theater. We started looking for locations.

I remained insistently idealistic about the importance of my associate's creative contribution — whose tastes and sense of style were very different from mine — and so I allowed my own concept for the store to change. The following summer we opened. Although it now seems incredible to me, what we ended up with was the kind of shop I had all my life detested: a fancy, trendy, expensive boutique. A business with which, at heart, I had nothing in common.

And, as if this weren't enough, the *location, location, location* was bad, bad, bad. Our shop was situated in the rear section of a newly built, little country mall. The parking lot, though not paved, was covered with a surface — called airport mix — which, we were told, would be just as adequate. In the spring, while we were working to set up the shop, a customer coming to the store next door to us stepped out of her car and sank up to her shins in mud. Others had to be carried or helped to walk on boards to the brick pavement that ran in front of the building. People stayed away in droves.

On our opening night we threw a party. It was an ominous beginning. Our investors came, as did many of our friends. Everyone tried hard to find nice things to say, but in fact the store was starkly unfinished. The carpet was not yet down and there was little inventory on the shelves. At one point in the evening, our contractor asked our banker's wife to dance. Before it was over, he had inadvertently broken her nose.

Sales were dismal. With what little revenues we had going to defray bank debt, there was not enough to keep up our inventory. I had fights with the bank, exchanged threats with creditors. It got to the point where I began to refuse to answer the phone. My associate and I started to squabble. Money ran out. She left. We raised a little more money. We lost that. We ran sales, we held events. All our frantic activity produced nothing but the appearance of coping. Slowly, inexorably, it all collapsed. Failure, no option. I couldn't deny it this time.

Panic and confusion set in. My personal life — completely enmeshed as it was with the business — showed signs of the strain. I was drinking aggressively, downing several beer steins of rum and tonic in a potent 60/40 dose, every night after the store closed. I was sleeping badly, eating large and heavy meals. I grew sheepish among friends and bearish at home. Jennifer and I began to fight. Without realizing it, I was endangering both my health — which I had never much cared about — and my family — which I cared about intensely.

Two events signaled both the peak of my crisis and the beginning of change. One was an ultimatum from my wife. If I wanted my family to remain intact, I had to make changes, immediately. The other occurred one day in my pastor's office. While telling him about everything that was going on, I suddenly heard a clear and desperate voice within me turn to God and say, "I can't do it anymore. You do it!" I felt an instant response, a sense that an enormous burden was being lifted off my shoulders. This was the turning point. This was an experience that allowed me for a moment to see my own inauthentic and alienated self in relation to something infinitely greater. It was, in the worst hour of crisis, again an experience of connectedness. I had been there before, of course, but not since long ago, as a child, sitting on a pier on the coast of Maine under a starlit sky.

The next year was a long, slow process of dismantling the person that I had allowed myself to become and the travesty of a life that person had falsely built around him. I began instinctively by acknowledging my failure, though I did not know then what to call this crucial stage. The first task was to close the company. One by one, I met with the shareholders and let them know that their investments were irrecoverable. I held a final clearance, negotiated with bankers, sought whatever breaks I could get from our creditors, loaded whatever merchandise and store fixtures we could not liquidate into the back of a borrowed truck and drove away. All this was done in a state of numbness, with a feeling that none of this was real, that I was somehow moving through a dream. Looking back on this period from the safety of the present, I suspect that this alienation was caused by my sudden realization — brought on by this inescapable failure — that I had no idea who I was. It felt as though I had at some time or another now long since past misplaced myself. At worst though, for me as for most people who fail, the "self" having trouble was a "body-double" standing in for the true self waiting in the wings.

While I was working through this dilemma, I signed on with a small advertising and public relations company that Jennifer had set up. I tried to make myself useful and, in the process, discovered a new interest in personal and organizational development. I found that I was good at observing how people in other companies interacted, affecting — and being affected by — patterns of relationships and communication. All these, I saw, were rooted to deeper questions of self-image values and what today I would call "operational theologies." More importantly, I found that I could be of service. By the end of the year I resolved to go to Andover Newton Theological School to study pastoral counseling.

This last decision was made, not with any clear career objective in mind, but out of a sense that through my struggle with success and failure I had come face to face with common but important problems in our society. I turned to theological education to help me find the answers woven into the connections between my own experience and the experience of others. I cannot claim my progress in this has been steady. There have been reversals and detours. At one point, to raise cash I even took a job as a business manager! Nevertheless, with the passage of time, life, which before had only become more and more senseless, was now richer, more meaningful, and, not incidentally, more whole and balanced. While the cash flow some months may still be a struggle, everything else has improved — health, work, relationships, peace of mind.

For me the greatest irony of all was being invited to write this book. For by committing my misadventures to paper, by raising the questions which lie behind the stress and confusion each one of us faces as we try to cope with life, I am putting this experience of failure to work. Today, Jennifer and I run a workshop practice that features seminars on transforming failure and finding a vision for one's life work. We know and we tell people that the questions we raise about failure are more important than any specific answers our experience might have generated thus far. We are limited experts at best. It has been a tremendous source of satisfaction to us that many people appreciate the work we do and that we have the opportunity to help individuals who are having a hard time. It is too early to tell whether or not our practice will be "successful" from a business point of view. But it is clear that each of us is much closer to living out an authentic vision for our life's work.

My own story raises questions about the experience of failure that have led me in the direction of religion to search for answers. The revelation in the pastor's office and my subsequent decision to go to seminary are expressions of the spiritual reality I perceived was beginning to take shape. To tell my story in any other fashion — to shift the description of the lessons I learned to a psychological model, for instance — would not accurately reflect the truth of my experience as it unfolded for me. However, in interviewing others in the course of our research we did not discover a consensus about the role of spirituality in the failure crisis: there was no common response to crisis that took the shape of renewed interest in religion or spirituality.

This is not to say, however, that there were no common conclusions. Everybody we spoke with emerged from their individual crises with a way of looking at the world that was markedly different from the view that predominated — if unconsciously — prior to their experience of failure. Individuals we spoke with felt that through failing, their understanding of themselves and the world had been *expanded*, not diminished, in significant ways. Some did find this through a new religious understanding. Others simply discovered in a secular sense a richer and more meaningful way of life. Which is preferable? Is one "the goal" and the other merely a stage along the way? It is not the purpose of this book to answer questions such as these (although it is probably clear which view I personally believe). What is important and relevant to this exploration is that to experience failure honestly and openly is to encounter oneself — and life itself — in a way that can be uniquely rewarding. And even though these rewards may be shrouded with problems, few other experiences contain this promise.

NOTES

Introduction

1. Joseph Campbell, *Hero with A Thousand Faces*, Bolligen, Princeton University Press, Princeton, NJ, 1973, p. 30. Campbell (1904 – 1987), was an internationally acclaimed scholar and lecturer on mythology, who wrote many influential books; among them are the popular PBS-TV tie-in, *The Power of Myth* (with Bill Moyers).

Chapter 1, The Problem and Promise of Failure

1. From a letter to W. Lutoslawski, May 6, 1906. In *Bartlett's Familiar Quotations*, Little, Brown & Co., 1980.

Chapter 2, Failure and Society

1. Robert Bly, National Book Award-winning poet from Minnesota, has written several nonfiction books on psychology and myth. Among them are the best seller *Iron John: A Book About Men*, published by Addison-Wesley, 1990, and *A Little Book on the Human Shadow*, published by Harper & Row, 1988. Bly is also a leader of workshops on the meanings of maleness in contemporary life.

2. Robert N. Bellah, et al, *Habits of the Heart: Individualism and Commitment in American Life*, Harper & Row, 1985, p. 145.

3. Birch and Rasmussen, *The Predicament of the Prosperous*,

Westminster Press, Philadelphia, 1978, pp. 44-45.

4. *Coping with Failure*, eds. Greinacher and Mette, Stiching Concilium & SMC Press/Trinity Press International, 1990, Editorial, p. *ix*.

5. Dr. Bruce A. Baldwin, "Marital Materialism," *USAir Magazine*, April 1991, pp. 76-86.

Chapter 3, Failure and the Individual

1. Wendy Williams, *The Power Within*, Harper & Row, 1990, pp. 28-29.

2. Harold Kushner, *When Bad Things Happen to Good People*, Avon Books, NY 1981, p. 3.

3. Georgess McHargue, *The Beasts of Never*, Delacorte Press, NY, 1988, pp. 29-31.

Chapter 4, Three Common Areas for Failure

1. Judith Harkness Richardson, "Sizer on school reform: Let's rethink the basics," *Boston Sunday Globe*, March 32, 1991, pp. A16-17.

2. Victor Frankl, from *The Doctor and the Soul*, Vintage, NY, 1986, p. 117.

Chapter 5, Failure as Threefold Process

1. Erika Schuchardt, "Coping With Failure 'Why Me?' Opportunities for Learning to Live," from *Coping With Failure*, eds. Greinacher and Mette, Stiching Concilium & SMC Press/Trinity Press International, 1990, pp. 59-79.

2. Charles V. Gerkin, *Crisis Experience in Modern Life*, Abingdon Press, Nashville, 1979, pp. 32-33.

3. Judith Viorst, *Necessary Losses: The loves, illusions, dependencies and impossible expectations that all of us have to give up in order to grow*, Simon & Schuster, New York, 1986.

The Author's Story

1. Cassette Tape, "The Human Shadow," by Robert Bly, © Robert Bly, 1989. Sound Horizons, Audio Video, Inc., New York.

2. C. S. Lewis, *The Discarded Image*, Cambridge University Press, London, 1964, pp. 98-99.

SUGGESTED READING

All the evidence we need to illustrate the point that Americans do not like to think about failure is readily available in the Subject Guide to *Books in Print*. Looking up both "Failure" and "Success," you'll find that there are almost 750 titles listed under "Success" alone, and this is without counting the titles of related books in twelve cross-referenced subcategories. Under "Failure" there are nine (that's right: 9) titles altogether. The ratio is 83:1. Thinking seriously about the positive benefits of failure qualifies you as something of a pioneer. Welcome.

Here are some suggestions for further reading.

Bergson, Henri, *The Creative Mind,,* transla. Mabelle L. Andison, Greenwood Press, 1968.
Bly, Robert, *Iron John: A Book About Men.* Addison-Wesley Publishing Company, 1991.
Bolles, Richard N., *The Three Boxes of Life: And How to Get Out of Them.* Ten Speed Press, 1981.

Borysenko, Joan, *Mending the Body, Mending the Mind.* Addison-Wesley, 1987.

Boynton, Sandra, *Don't Let the Turkeys Get You Down.* Workman Press, 1986.

Bradshaw, John, *Bradshaw On: The Family - A Revolutionary Way of Self-Discovery.* Health Communications, Inc., 1988.

Crum, Thomas F., *The Magic of Conflict: Turning a Life of Work into a Work of Art.* Simon & Schuster, 1988.

Crystal, John C., & Bolles, Richard N., *Where Do I Go From Here With My Life?* ("A very systematic, practical, and effective life/work planning manual for students of all ages, instructors, counselors, career seekers and career changers.") Ten Speed Press, 1980.

Dail, Hilda Lee, *The Lotus and the Pool: How to Create Your Own Career.* Shambhala, 1989.

Eliot, T. S., *The Complete Poems and Plays,* 1909–1950, Harcourt Brace & World, 1952.

Fields, Rick, et al, *Chop Wood, Carry Water: A Guide To Feeling Spiritual Fulfillment in Everyday Life.* J. P. Tarcher, 1984.

Frankl, Viktor E., *Man's Search for Meaning.* Washington Square Press, 1963.

Gershon, David & Straub, Gail, *Empowerment: The Art of Creating Your Life As You Want It.* Delacorte, 1989.

Greenleaf, Robert, *Servant Leadership: A Journey into the Nature of Legitimate Power & Greatness.* Paulist Press, 1977.

Greinacher, Norbert and Mette, Norbert, Eds., *Coping With Failure.* Concilium, SCM Press, Trinity Press International, 1990.

Hanh, Thich Nhat, *The Miracle of Mindfulness.* Beacon Press, Boston, 1988.

Hyatt, Carol & Gottlieb, Linda, *When Smart People Fail: Rebuilding Yourself for Success*. Penguin, 1988.

Kushner, Harold, *When All You've Ever Wanted Isn't Enough*: *The Search for a Life that Matters*. Pocket Books, 1990.

Nelson, James B., *The Intimate Connection: Male Sexuality, Masculine Spirituality*. The Westminster Press, 1988.

O'Connor, Elizabeth, *Cry Pain, Cry Hope: Thresholds to Purpose & Creativity*. Word Books, 1987.

Palmer, Parker, *The Active Life: A Spirituality of Work, Creativity & Caring*. Harper & Row, 1990.

Peck, George & Hoffman, John S., eds., *The Laity in Ministry*. Judson Press, 1984.

Pile, Stephen, *Cannibals in the Cafeteria And Other Fabulous Failures*. Harper & Row, 1990.

Sheehy, Gail, *Passages: Predictable Crises of Adult Life*. Bantam Books, 1984.

Also *Pathfinders: Overcoming the Crises of Adult Life and Finding Your Own Path to Well-Being*. Bantam Books, 1982.

Sher, Barbara, *Wishcraft: How to Get What You Really Want*. Ballantine Books, 1979.

Sinetar, Marsha, *Do What You Love, The Money Will Follow: Discovering Your Right Livelihood*. Dell, 1989.

Steele, Bill, *The Need to Fail*. Ann Arbor Press, 1974.

"*Amazing, three failed marriages, scores of disastrous relationships, many financial reversals, and countless physical ailments, but through it all I've always had good luck parking.*"

Drawing by Mankoff; © 1989
The New Yorker Magazine, Inc.

ABOUT THE AUTHORS

John Lord is pursuing an advanced degree in vocational counseling at Andover-Newton Theological Seminary, Newton Center, MA. His work with individuals and organizations, along with his varied experience in public relations and theater, has uniquely equipped him for his work as co-director, with his wife, **Jennifer Walker Lord**, of The Life Project, a center for failure experience workshops and vocational counseling.

Jeffrey Wold, M.D., is a psychiatrist in Stockbridge, MA, where, for twelve years, he was a staff member at the Austen Riggs Center. In addition to serving as an instructor in psychiatry at Harvard University, Cambridge Hospital Residency Program, he is also a consulting psychiatrist and clinical supervisor at Wellspring, a residential treatment center for adolescents and adults in Bethlehem, CT. Dr. Wold has written on the problem of adolescent delinquency and is at work on a book about the anxiety associated with separation.